RAISE YOUR GAME
HOW TO SPEAK FLUENT SPORT

For G, with all my love

RAISE YOUR GAME

HOW TO SPEAK FLUENT SPORT

IAN VALENTINE

CARTOONS BY OLIVER PRESTON

Quiller

Copyright © Ian Valentine (text) 2016
Copyright © Oliver Preston (illustrations) 2016

First published in the UK in 2016 by Quiller, an imprint of Quiller Publishing Ltd

British Library Cataloguing-in-Publication Data
A catalogue record for this book is available from the British Library

ISBN 978 1 84689 233 2

Book design and jacket design by Sharyn Troughton
Printed in the Czech Republic

Quiller

An imprint of Quiller Publishing Ltd

Wykey House, Wykey, Shrewsbury, SY4 1JA
Tel: 01939 261616 Fax: 01939 261606
E-mail: info@quillerbooks.com
Website: www.quillerpublishing.com

CONTENTS

INTRODUCTION

WHAT IS IT ABOUT SPORT THAT GRABS US by the eyeballs and won't let go? If you've ever flicked over to Wimbledon to catch the score, then lost the whole afternoon to a five set thriller or found yourself yelling at the telly when a player missed a tackle, putt, straight delivery or open goal; then you know about sport's bewitching power and what it is to get carried off by sport's rip tide. It's not just about the Djokovics, Messis and McIlroys of this world either. To witness a family member or friend do the best they can – whether in victory or defeat – is to ride sport's emotional rollercoaster.

Watching sport may be no more than a welcome distraction after a busy day or week – an easy dose of escapism and entertainment like a rom com, quiz show or cookery competition. But it has the power to cut way deeper. Sport can affect us in ways that we rarely experience. We find genuine inspiration in the acts of exceptional men and women who are pushing new limits of human skill and physicality. Or, and this often tugs at the heartstrings harder, we feel ourselves uplifted by individuals and teams that perform at the keenest edge of their ability, tasting success (or falling agonisingly short) in a way that we never forget. Their 'one shot' at glory is all the more exhilarating. Having lived their journey, we are emboldened to stretch ourselves to overcome our own challenges.

Sport can hurt so badly too, and not just physically. If you invest emotionally in a player or team, then you must be prepared to endure crushing disappointment along the way. Should your hero or club slump into an extended run of poor form, or get embroiled in scandal, then your loyalty will be tested to breaking point. Whether you wear the stripes of Barcelona or Shrewsbury Town, you're striped for life. For every celebrating fan, there is another poor soul rueing cruel twists of fate, close shaves and costly errors. Just as the highlights burn long in the memory, so the painful losses are impossible to erase. Yet, with every fresh twist, we find ourselves caring more than before.

As Leicester City supporters will confirm – it's worth believing, no matter the odds.

Sport helps us feel part of something bigger. We're witnessing a moment in time, often with millions of others. We can say we saw it happen. Immediately, there's a bond with whoever saw it too. This is equally true if you watch your son, mum or best mate do something on a sports field for the first time. Hearing about it later is never quite the same.

There is undoubtedly a voyeuristic element to being a sports spectator. Nobody wants a downhill skier to catch an edge at 80 mph, but we know one of the field probably will, and this ghoulish fascination only adds to the viewing excitement. Penalty shoot-outs in football are arguably an unsatisfactory way of splitting two well-matched teams, but they make for some of the best drama in sport. Watching superstars buckle under unimaginable pressure and then dissolve into floods of tears is all part of the spectacle.

Of course, you don't need to know everything about a sport to gain enjoyment from watching it played. Just like a wine, film score, painting or pudding, we can all appreciate a good match or race without knowing its backstory. Yet, a little extra knowledge here and there will intensify your experience hugely. Sticking with wine, music, art and cookery for a moment, sport has likewise hatched a rich dictionary of terms that set pictures floating through the minds of those who understand them. Being a fluent sport speaker gives you access to heated conversations at the local pub or the office water cooler. The right vocabulary offers a much fuller experience of matches from the comfort of your sofa, the hubbub of the stands or the dog-eat-dog environment of the school touchline. Who knows, a choice phrase or crafted insight might even prick the ears of your boss… or future spouse?

Of course, if you can't talk sport then conversations amongst certain friends can be tedious. Match commentaries sound like garbled Italian – there are occasional words and phrases that are somewhat familiar, but the overall meaning is lost. Whole sections of the newspaper are written in this peculiar dialect. It may be clear that such-and-such won and that what's-her-name played well. But as to how it happened? Well, that's still a bit of a mystery.

I've had the sports bug for as long as I can remember. Someone once said the definition of a cricket lover is a person who can't walk past a match without watching an over bowled, even if it's just some kids playing in the street. For me, that would be true for any sport – I don't think I could ignore a game of street hockey, boules or even dominoes for that matter. I've tried my hand wherever possible and been fortunate to write regularly about sport, and watch some remarkable moments, all of which I fondly include in my most vivid life memories.

The idea for *Raise Your Game* came from a conversation with a friend who said that while he enjoyed following Six Nations rugby, he wasn't entirely sure why half the decisions were given or what the commentators were talking about. Not long after, I found myself watching a stage of the Tour de France and realising that, yes, I was gripped, but there were others who were enjoying it at a far deeper level. They could see a bigger picture that I could not. And they knew what all the quirky French terms meant. If only I had a layman's description with a few choice definitions, I might see the wood for the trees.

My aim is to celebrate each of these sports' unique charms and language, offering plenty of pointers and phrases to lift your viewing to another level, whether you are an occasional enthusiast or card-carrying addict. I am pleased to report that I am not as tragic as I once thought. Indeed, I had only ever skimmed the surface of sports such as water polo, basketball or sumo. In the past, I might have passed up Olympic events such as Greco-Roman wrestling, handball or Modern Pentathlon – but now I will set a reminder.

I certainly never knew that that elite croquet players use two balls instead of one. Or that a *bonk* is bad in cycling but good in snowboarding. Or that Olympic weightlifting is basically a glorified game of chicken. Or that a *dog's eye with lashings of dead horse* is the highlight of an Aussie Rules match. I can't wait to ask for one, when I get the chance.

All of the sports are summarised, providing an easy companion to watch the action. A glossary of useful and colourful terms will also bring the sports to life, and help translate the commentators and columnists. With such a vast number of sports in the world, each with a gazillion terms and curiosities, the prospect of writing *The Definitive Guide to Sports Language* didn't appeal. I've chosen those sports that I personally wanted to learn more about (e.g. sumo);

sports that offer interesting jargon (e.g. Aussie Rules); and events that I feel will prove most appealing in terms of 'watchability' (e.g. Le Tour de France). In other words, it's entirely subjective.

When picking which terms to include, I was drawn to expressions that best help to explain the sport, and also those that raise a smile or display keen-edged wit, usually on the part of a long-forgotten spectator or journalist. Again, you'll see that the definitions aren't presented in alphabetical order – they are written to be read and enjoyed. I deliberately shied away from writing a reference book or dictionary. Throughout, I have been endlessly impressed by sport's ability to capture a moment with the right word or killer phrase. Slang is definitely alive and kicking in sport.

Talking of deft touches, I am thrilled that Oliver Preston has drawn the cartoons for this book. Just like a reader, the first thing I'll do when I see a copy is leaf through to see his razor sharp observations.

I hope you enjoy reading the words too. Whether you're a *hack* or a *gun*, hit the *giraffe* or *caterpillar*, smack a *Ken Livingstone* or *Jean Marie Le Pen*, ride *fakie* or *goofy* (or both), play *handshake* or *penhold*, I wish you good sport at every turn.

TOUR DE FRANCE

THE OVERALL CHAMPION is the fastest to cycle 3,500 miles around France. Set over 23 days, the Tour is split into 21 stages, which are competitive races in their own right, usually decided by a sprint finish. The winner needs to be a good all-rounder, capable of excelling in both the flatter and gruelling mountain stages. The current leader of the race wears the yellow jersey, so it may well change hands several times. However, it's not just about winning the Tour, especially as the major contenders can't go flat out every day and may spend long periods coasting in the *peloton* (the main body of riders). Claiming individual stages is hugely prestigious, so the specialist sprinters are also big stars, while opportunistic breakaways from the *peloton* keep the excitement bubbling. The leading sprinter wears the green jersey, while the best climber (King of the Mountain) sports the red polka dot jersey. There are typically 22 teams of nine riders, and the tour is as much about teamwork and tactics, as pace and endurance. The champion won't cross the line fastest in Paris without the help of his *domestiques*, who do a lot of his donkey and dirty work. Beware: for such a long race, the Tour is addictive viewing.

Talk a good game

L'Auto: The magazine that founded the Tour in 1903 as a publicity stunt.

Grand Tours: The three leading multi-stage races: the Tour de France, Giro D'Italia and La Vuelta a Espana.

General classification (GC): The overall times for the riders during a multi-stage race. The current leader of the GC wears the yellow jersey.

Peloton: The massed group of cyclists that sits in behind the stage leaders.

Autobus: The mass of riders at the back of the race in the mountain stages, usually the sprinters and other non-climbers. Also known as the *bus* or the *laughing group*, their aim is simply to finish within the time limit and avoid being *swept up*.

Team leader: The star rider and the team's best chance of winning the overall race, a jersey or a stage. Everyone else in the team is meant to work for him.

Parcours: French word for the route of each stage.

Bonking: To run out of juice and grind to a halt. Also called *exploding; cracking; popping; the hunger knock;* and *hitting the wall.*

Cadence: The rate in revolutions per minute at which the rider turns the pedals.

Time trial: An individual race against the clock (*contre-la-montre* in French) or *race of truth*, as the leaders are out on their own. May have a big bearing on the overall result.

Hour record: This isn't part of the Tour, but it has involved many of the Tour's finest riders. Dating back to the 1870s, the contender has 60 minutes to cover as much distance as possible. Since then, the record has stretched from 26km to over 54km (at the time of writing). As ever with cycling, its history is chequered by controversy related to doping and disagreements over equipment.

Directeur Sportif: The team gaffer, who decides on the tactics for each stage.

Domestique: Dogsbody, worker bee – the team leader can't win without them. They feed and water the star rider, taking it in turns to act as a wind barrier, or to chase down and block opponents.

Rouleur: Also known as *super-domestiques*, they set the pace for the team and *provide a wheel* for the team leader over long distances.

Sprinter: You don't have to be mad to be a sprinter, but it sure helps. Speed is half the battle. The best can also ghost their way through a mass of opponents, all pedal to the metal at 50 mph. The lead sprinter wears the green jersey on the Tour de France. Watch out for the rainbow jersey too – if the rider is the road race world champion.

Lead-out man: Another unsung hero, who provides a wheel for the sprinter to follow. Riding in his slipstream, the sprinter then bursts forward in the final moments of the race.

Bunch sprint: The mass dash for the line at the end of a stage by the specialist sprinters and their lead-out men.

Hors catégorie (HC): Mountain climbs are rated 1–4, with 1 the hardest. Those that are even steeper are deemed *HC*. Legendary mountain climbs include the pitiless Mont Ventoux and the vicious hairpins of L'Alpe d'Huez.

Climber: A rider with high power-to-weight ratio who relishes *HC* inclines. The race is often won or lost in the mountains. The lead climber wears the red polka dot jersey, and the best climber for that year is named *King of the Mountains.*

Lanterne rouge: Named after the red light at the rear of a train, this is the GC backmarker. Not an insult, as competing in and finishing the tour is no mean feat.

Musette: A small cloth shoulder bag with food and *bidons* (water bottles). Once the rider has refilled his pockets, the *musette* is tossed to one side.

Piano: To ride at a quiet pace and conserve energy.

Breakaway: A small group of riders who attack during a stage, often to gain publicity for their team sponsors. They are usually caught by the pack (which can move up to 10 seconds per kilometre quicker), although some are left to fight it out. It's the breakaways that make concentrating on your work difficult, if you're following the stage at your computer.

Bridge: To make up a gap, either with the breakaway ahead or the peloton when lagging behind.

Drop: To leave a rider or riders behind you.

Draft: To benefit from the pocket of still air behind the rider in front, either to save energy or to launch an attack. By staying within a bike's length, the follower saves up to 40 per cent of their energy, as they don't fight air resistance. With riders wheel to wheel, all drafting each other, the peloton pile-ups are inevitable and spectacular!

'As far as I can see, it's the same bunch of bums that came through here last year.'

Work: To put in a shift at the lead of a group, allowing others to draft. Also called *pulling*.

Leech: A rider who's happy to draft others, but won't work in return. The French call them *rats*. Not a good reputation to gain. Also known as *wheelsucking*.

Pétard mouillé: The French for a damp squib. To attack without success.

Faire dégueuler sa bouillie: French slang (literally, to puke your porridge) for a rider who is busting a gut.

Danseuse: Riding out of the saddle, dancing from side to side in a tall gear.

Pedal with your ears: Another French insult, meaning to cycle unstylishly, with your head bobbing left and right.

Au pain et à l'eau claire: To cycle on bread and clear water, i.e. naturally, without drugs.

Saler la soupe: To salt the soup – a French euphemism for taking performance-enhancing drugs.

À bloc: To ride flat out. To *hammer*.

Props: Congratulations, kudos, due respect. The French might say '*chapeau!*', as in – to doff one's cap at someone out of respect.

Bacon: Grazes and cuts caused by sliding on tarmac. Also called *road rash*. With nasty crashes unavoidable, you can't be a top class rider unless you can pedal through the pain barrier.

Panache: A rider who shows courage or adventure, often after a crash or injury. *Chapeau!*

Bike throw: Sounds like a tantrum, but it's the lunge for the line by a sprinter.

Blocking: When members of a team slow the tempo of rivals, usually to help their teammates in a break.

Grand Départ: The opening stage(s) of Le Tour. It now takes place in venues outside of France, for example Yorkshire.

Brick: A rider who is good at descending, but a weak climber. *Descendre comme une caisse à savon* (literally, descend like a soapbox) is to fly down like you're riding a go-kart and without consideration for others.

Kite: The opposite of a brick.

Fumer le pipe: Smoking a pipe. On top form. To pedal with no sign of fatigue, while everyone else is puffing.

Caravane: The team support cars behind the *peloton* and the commercial bandwagon in front.

Étape: A stage. There are 21 in Le Tour. For teams that don't have a star rider capable of winning the overall race, then stage wins are still prestigious. Legendary Belgian rider Eddy Merckx currently has the most with 34 wins.

Flamme rouge: A red flag displayed with one kilometre remaining from the finish line of a stage, usually suspended above the road.

Les Pavés: Several stages are renowned – and feared – for their slippery cobbles. Rain can cause havoc.

Count the cobbles: To ride painfully slowly as a result of exhaustion.

Gap: A space between riders that negates drafting. Also used as a verb. For example, he gapped his opponent.

Kick: Accelerate with a few pedal turns to create a gap.

Join the mafia: To collude with a member of a different team on a shared goal, such as blocking or riding down an opponent. Alliances can be short-lived, but live long in the memory…

Magic spanner: When the mechanics pretend to be fixing a rider's bike on the move, but they're really giving him a chance to hold onto the car and take a breather.

Sticky bottle: Another cunning energy-saving technique, whereby the rider holds onto a drinks bottle held out of a car. After a couple of seconds, they risk punishment from the all-powerful *commissaires*.

Door prize: Smacking into the open door of a parked car. Oof!

Squirrel: A rider with a bad reputation for swerving or decelerating suddenly. Nobody wants to draft them.

Vultures: The ghoulish spectators who head to the areas where a bad crash is most likely to happen.

MAMIL: Middle-aged Men In Lycra – a salesman's dream.

Fred: Insult to a rider who is out of their depth (often a MAMIL with all the gear but no idea).

Granny gear: The lowest gear. Perfect for climbing mountains.

Gutter bunny: Pejorative term for a city commuter.

FOOTBALL

TO WIN A GAME OF FOOTBALL, at some point you're going to need to score more goals than your opponents. But in reality, very little time in a match is actually spent scoring goals. Most of the 90 minutes is passed trying to put a player in a space with the ball where they have a chance of beating the keeper, and stopping your opponents from creating opportunities of their own. As such, football is often won by out-thinking the other team – finding and exploiting its weaknesses, and imposing your game plan. Of course, teams that play in several different styles are the most difficult to wear down and find sufficient ways to score at the other end.

At the top level, even the worst teams in the league will usually limit the best sides to three or four. Perhaps that's part of football's thrill – goals are hard to come by, so every success is rightly celebrated by players and fans alike. Attack-minded teams with the aim of 'scoring one more than you' are exciting to watch, but often get caught out. Defensive teams that are happy to win 1–0 are less entertaining, although their fans are quick to forgive if they keep grinding out the results. Of course, the best teams can do it all. They're solid at the back, competitive in midfield, blessed with strikers who regularly find the back of the net, and they can 'win ugly' if needs be. A decent manager and backroom staff, who second guess the oppo and get the team playing for each other, will often prove the difference in a close encounter.

Confidence and teamwork, or lack of it, plays a huge role in football. Getting on a good run – whether as a striker scoring goals, or a team in the league or in a cup – can take a lesser club or nation on to achieve extraordinary feats. Squads without the household names can punch above their weight, relying on hard work, fitness, good discipline and a strategic game plan. Likewise, a squad of superstars will fall from grace spectacularly if they can't gel or their heads go down. And every opposition fan will love it!

Of course, football runs much deeper than hoofing or nutting a ball into a net. Local and national tribalism is central to the sport's appeal. While it is tempting to knock the vast sums of money lavished on the world's top players, there's no denying their importance to the lives of thousands of people, who track (and dissect) their every move.

Talk a good game

Formation: How the 10 outfield players line up on paper, with defenders, midfielders and strikers. For example, 4–4–2 or 3–4–3.

In goal: To be the goalkeeper, the only player allowed to handle the ball deliberately. Aside from courage, cat-like athleticism and a loud voice, most keepers have the mental strength to cope with long periods of doing precious little save getting stick from the away fans.

Keeper had no chance: When a shot is so good, it's unstoppable. Or the ball took a wicked deflection. The keeper can do nothing but pick the ball out of the net.

A screamer: A hard strike or volley from distance that flies into the top corner of the net.

A sitter: A poor miss. He should have buried it.

Transfer Window: The official FIFA-sanctioned registration period when players can move from one club to another. Most transfers will happen in the pre-season window, but there's an additional mid-season window, when struggling managers go begging to their chairman for a new striker. Clubs often complete their horse-trading in the final hours before the window closes.

Offside trap: When the 'back four' stand in a line and move forward together, to catch an attacker offside behind them. If they mistime it, or one defender lags behind, then the striker is played onside and runs through on goal.

Move the goalposts: Not something the players can do, but politicians find it very easy.

FOOTBALL

'Here we go, son. The transfer window's opened.'

Clean sheet: To stop the opposition from scoring all match.

Three points: A win in the league is usually worth three points. A draw gets you one. 'We'll take the three points' is a good way to defend a scrappy performance. To *drop points* often implies teams have drawn or lost a match they ought to have won.

Park the bus: To score first, then pull all your players back to defend your lead. Similar to the Italian *Catenaccio* (door bolt) strategy to win 1–0. Teams that are happy with a point might park the bus from the start.

Total Football: Made famous by the Dutch in the 1970s, this flowing strategy relies on every player being able to play in every position, with an equal ability to pass, dribble, defend, etc.

Do a Leicester: To win the league against all odds, or (more generally) achieve a fairy tale success. Reference to the Leicester City side who comfortably won the 2015–2016 English Premier League, despite starting the season as 5000–1 rank outsiders.

The wall: To defend free kicks, a line of players will stand between the striker and the goal, 10 metres away. To stop them encroaching, the ref will mark the line with vanishing spray.

Dead ball specialist: A player who is good at taking free kicks, corners and penalties (i.e. when the ball isn't moving). Some teams rely heavily on earning these opportunities to score, as they can launch moves straight off the training ground.

Box-to-box midfielder: A tenacious player with a good engine, and the ability to attack and defend. Usually spends the match running from one penalty box to the other.

Dive: To simulate that you've been fouled. If done well, you could win a penalty or get an opponent booked. If the ref doesn't buy it, then you'll likely be booked yourself and roundly jeered. A reputation for being a diver is hard to shift. Fans don't forget.

Gone down like he's shot: Another type of play-acting. When the slightest touch in the penalty box causes a 75 kg action man to fold like a rag doll.

Feint: To dribble the ball at an opponent and send them the wrong way by dropping a shoulder. Also to *shimmy*.

Poacher: A striker who loiters about the penalty box and scores a lot of goals. Worth their weight in gold to the club. Probably more.

Goalazo: What excitable Spanish commentators shout when a spectacular goal is scored. 'Gooooooaaaaaalllllllllllaaaaaaazzzooooo!!!!!'

Group of Death: There's always one qualifying group in a major tournament that has one too many big teams. To escape a Group of Death is an achievement in itself. The *minnows* in the group are likely to be eaten up.

Lose the dressing room: When a team stops 'playing for the gaffer' and starts doing their own thing on the pitch. Some managers get the support of the board. Most don't.

Maestro: Usually a forward midfielder, who pulls the strings with clever passes and deft touches.

Nutmeg: When a players beats an opponent by nipping the ball between their legs. If they can shout 'megs!' as they do it, the humiliation is complete.

Olympic goal: To swerve the ball from a corner kick and score directly. Originally called the *gol olimpico*, when Argentinean Cesáreo Onzari scored against Uruguay in 1924. Uruguay had just won the Olympic gold and the name stuck.

Pedalada: To make several step-overs in an attempt to confuse the defender.

Own goal: When a member of the defending team accidentally puts the ball in their own net, usually as a deflection or when trying to clear the ball. In the UK, the *Dubious Goals Committee* will adjudge whether goals are own goals or should be credited to an attacker.

Panenka: A penalty chip kick, which floats in over the keeper after he has dived. Named after Czech Antonin Panenka. Looks great if it works.

Penalty shootout: When the scoreline is still tied after regular time and overtime, the match is decided on penalties. Selecting players from the eleven that finishes the match, each team has up to five attempts to beat the keeper by taking a shot at goal from the penalty spot. If it's tied after five, then they go to sudden death. Pundits will say that it's a shame that the match should become a lottery. But there's no beating a shoot-out for drama.

Rabona: To wrap your leg round your standing foot to strike the ball. Basically, kicking the ball with your legs crossed. It goes back to 1948, when an Argentinean goal machine called Ricardo Infante was credited as its inventor. A magazine wrote a headline saying 'Infante bunks off school'. To bunk off is *rabona* in Spanish, and the name caught on.

Seal dribble: To head the ball forward to yourself.

Silky: A player with *tricky* skills. Great at technical stuff like dribbling, free kicks, trapping the ball, etc.

Sombrero: To pass a player by knocking the ball over their 'hat'.

Tiki-taka: Made famous by Barcelona and Spain, this is fast one-touch short passing, with plenty of one-twos, give-and-goes and movement off the ball. The idea is to pass the ball into the net and generally run your opponents ragged.

Yo-yo club: A team that goes up and down in the league – promoted one year, demoted the next, then straight back up, and so on.

By Mutual Consent: What the club says when they've sacked the manager. Also: 'we've sat down and *come to an agreement.*'

Prawn Sandwich Brigade: The corporate boxes.

Hairdryer treatment: When the manager gives the team an earful at halftime. Made famous by Sir Alex Ferguson at Manchester United, who was more than happy to offer some of the world's best players a piece of his mind.

Handbags: Vigorous shoving and posturing, without really fighting each other, as in *handbags at dawn.*

Managerial merry-go-round: These days, the boss doesn't get long to prove his worth before the board loses patience and they 'come to an agreement'. But all is not lost, the ousted manager will be taking up a newly sacked manager's position with a different club soon enough.

Swapsies: To swap football stickers with your mates. Also when clubs swap players in real life.

Gaffer: The manager.

What's in a name?

Soccer.
Why is it that we say 'football' and the North Americans say 'soccer'?

Brits have played different forms of football for hundreds of years. Factors such as geography, fashion and class created rules that came and went. These rules included variations such as picking the ball up, tackling with legs or arms, and with all sorts of ways to score.

The Football Association formed in 1863, following the determination of a gritty Yorkshireman called Ebenezer Cobb Morley, now known as the father of modern football. He saw the need to codify a single sport, and make it distinct from the others, particularly rugby. In 1872, the first FA Cup was contested and eventually won by the Wanderers Club.

In the US and Canada, they developed their own national variations of football: American and Canadian Football. To differentiate, the word 'soccer' took root instead and comes from an abbreviated form of the official name 'Association Football'.

RUGBY UNION

ALTHOUGH RUGBY UNION IS TRADITIONALLY FIFTEENS (15-a-side), the simplest way to describe the aim of the game and its basic rules is to watch a game of Sevens (7-a-side). This simplified, all-action version is instantly entertaining for any spectators who don't yet know the sport.

The idea is to get the ball to other end of the pitch, either by kicking it or carrying it forward. Once there, you can score points by grounding the ball over the try line or by kicking the ball over the posts. Whoever scores the most points wins. You can't pass the ball forward and you mustn't tackle an opponent above the shoulders (or by tripping with your foot). Teams compete for restarts in scrums or line-outs. The winner is the team that creates space for runners to exploit and stops their opponents from doing the same. After watching one match, spectators are usually up to speed.

In Fifteens, with much less space to play in, there's more of an emphasis on team structure and technical ability. That's why you get such a discrepancy in the sizes of the players, from squat trolls, beanpoles and bulldozers to pocket rockets, show ponies and greyhounds. Different players are built for different aptitudes, although all modern professionals are expected to pass, tackle and force *turnovers*. Get them working in synch, and you have a team filled with power, speed, vision, courage and technical polish – incisive in attack, miserly in defence.

The downside, and it has become worse in recent years, is that rugby has a lot of rules. Spectators can be forgiven for not fully understanding the complexities of scrummaging, line-outs, rucks, mauls and the dreaded break-down. In rainy or scrappy games, usually dominated and decided by these technical aspects, the purists will purr with delight. But the occasional viewer who switched on for light relief may get frustrated or bored. It is something for the lawmakers to grapple with moving forward, but in the meantime, these phrases should help fill in the gaps.

What's in a name?

Try and conversion

In its simplest form, the aim of rugby is to score tries. Even at schoolboy or club level, scoring a try feels great, so heaven knows what it must be like to score for your country in front of a packed arena.

If a team grounds the ball over the opposition try line, then they score five points. Their kicker then has a chance to add another two points by converting the try – knocking the ball through the posts – from a point in line with where the try was scored. So if it was scored under the posts, the kick is right in front. If the try-scorer dotted down in the corner, then it's a touchline conversion.

In the early years of rugby (invented at Rugby School in 1823 when William Webb Ellis picked up the ball and ran, according to popular legend) the game was basically a free-for-all. Play revolved around a mass scrum, with vast teams of lads shoving, brawling and grappling to move the ball nearer the opposition's goal, with the aim of kicking a goal. Games could last for days without anyone scoring. If you did run in the ball over the line, then you could kick the ball to a teammate, who could *try* to score a goal (without being impeded). If he succeeded, then that was a converted try, which gained more points than the run in. Eventually, the try itself became more valuable than the conversion, but not until 1893.

Talk a good game

Forward pass: The ball can be thrown sideways or backwards, but never forward, otherwise a scrum is awarded to the opposition.

'Why don't YOU tell him to sit down and shut up?'

Overlap: This is when you have an extra man in the line, i.e. four attackers against three defenders. By *drawing your man* (forcing your opponent to tackle you and passing just before he does), you should be able to create space for the extra runner.

Turnover: This is what the commentator cries to alert the viewer that the opposition has pinched possession from the attacking team, usually in the breakdown, but also in a lineout or ripping the ball in open play. It's exciting, because the tables are suddenly turned, and players are now out of position, so the defensive team now has a golden opportunity to counter-attack before the opposition scramble their defence and align.

Offload: To pass the ball to a mate as you are tackled. Players that can *free the arms* and offload are invaluable gamebreakers. In a close match, just one brilliant offload can make all the difference.

The gainline: An imaginary line across the pitch, which shows if the attacking side has made any progress. A break, offload or rolling maul is a good way to 'cross the gainline' or 'get in behind the gainline'.

Maul: This loose scrum happens in open play, when the ball carrier is wrapped up with opposition players. Importantly, the ball must be *off the ground* for it to be a maul. Attacking players can use the maul to drive forward, shifting the ball to one another in a *rolling maul* – particularly effective from a line-out close to the opposition try line, where a short trundle can result in a 5-point *catch and drive*. If the opposition stops the ball coming back to the scrum half or going to ground to form a ruck, then they are awarded a scrum. So, the maul can be an unstoppable force or a frustrating way of coughing up possession, depending on how well it is drilled or how badly the opposition defend it.

Ruck: When a player is tackled, and he can't offload, he is meant to place the ball on the ground. As players join over the ball, a ruck is called by the referee and nobody is allowed to handle the ball until it comes out on their side. Usually, the attacking team will drive over the ball and play continues. Occasionally, the defending team *counter-rucks*, and gets the ball to pop out on their side. They then have a turnover. The verb *to ruck* describes the (mostly legal) act of climbing on an opponent on the wrong side and using your studs to stop them from interfering or slowing down the ball. It has all but dropped out of the game.

No hands!: What the ref shouts to tell players in a ruck to stop touching the ball. Also: *ball lost!* If a player ignores the ref, he will give away a penalty, and perhaps receive a yellow card if it was deemed cynical.

Phases: In open play, when the ball carrier is tackled, he can try to offload, so the attack can continue. If he can't, then he'll go to ground, hoping his teammates will create a ruck and recycle the ball. Then it's on to the next phase of the attack. With numerous rucks, a team can 'string phases together' and move up the pitch.

Breakdown: This is where modern rugby matches are often won and lost (along with spectators). When a player is tackled and hits the deck with the ball, there is a split second before the ruck is called by the referee (after which all players must let go of the ball). In this split second, a lot can and does happen. The attacking team will try to get over their man as quickly as possible, smash defenders away and set up a ruck. The defenders are allowed to try and pinch the ball, presuming they are onside and on their feet. Depending on the timing and execution – and most importantly the referee's interpretation of the breakdown – play will continue or a penalty will be awarded.

Jackal: When the defender goes in over the ball at the breakdown and tries to steal it. They must be on their feet. Indeed, the tackler can get back on his feet and pinch the ball if he is quick enough. This often happens when an attacker is isolated or his mates are 'slow to the breakdown'. It's all about timing – they could make a turnover or win a penalty, but also concede a penalty for handling in the ruck if too slow. As a partisan supporter, it's easy to think that the ref has got it wrong and penalised your team unjustly.

Holding on: When the tackled player is deemed to be stopping the defending side from making a legal turnover.

Discipline: A key part of modern rugby. Teams that can't resist handling the ball in the ruck or have a swing at their opponent will rack up a high penalty count and

invariably struggle to win the game. Ill-discipline is why few coaches have much hair.

Quick ball: The aim is to recycle the ball from rucks as quickly as possible, so you give opponents less time to reorganise their defensive line. Teams cherish the players who can *slow down* an opposition ball without getting penalised for it.

Play to the ref: This can mean two things. Firstly, it is *to play to the whistle* – as in don't stop playing just because the ref hasn't blown up. You may have seen a knock-on, but it doesn't mean he did. At the top level, it also means adapting to the referee's interpretation of the breakdown. Some refs favour attackers, others are quicker to reward the jackals. If a team doesn't adapt and feels hard done by, it won't do anything to change the score line.

Offside: There are two common types. Either, when you're in front of the ball when it's kicked and you push your luck by chasing it. Or when you're not behind the back feet of a scrum, ruck or maul, and you impact play.

Kicking for position: Territory is key, so the backs (usually the scrum half or fly half) will often try to kick the ball into the opposition half. A clearance kick is when you're defending and you need to get the ball out of play or far away from your try line. Forwards only kick in rare or comedy scenarios.

Garryowen: A high kick, which you chase and hope to catch first (usually before the full-back). Named after the Garryowen Club in Ireland, who used it to great effect in the 1920s. Also: an *up-and-under* or *bomb*.

High tackle: To scrag a player round the neck or head. Results in a penalty, and often a yellow card. Players can be red-carded if the high tackle is especially dangerous or reckless.

Late tackle: To smash a player after they have passed the ball. If the felon is deemed to have 'committed to the tackle', then he might get away with it, but it's usually pretty clear.

Tip tackle: To pick a player up and tip them backwards. The tackler must ensure the player doesn't fall dangerously. If they drive their opponent into the ground, that's a *spear tackle* and they'll probably get red-carded. If it's not spotted at the time, they can expect to be cited and then banned.

Tap tackle: To dive after a fleeing player and knock their heels together with your outstretched hand. Often saves a try.

Advantage: When the referee allows play to continue if the attacking team still

has possession after a misdemeanour by the opposition. If 'no advantage accrues' then they go back for the original offence. If the ref adjudges them to have gained sufficiently, then he'll shout 'advantage over! Again, it's open to his interpretation.

Cauliflower ears: Misshapen ears as a result of years in the scrum – a badge of honour for forwards.

Interception: When the defender reads a pass by the attacker and sprints away. If it's a prop, he might not get far. A winger will likely end up under the posts.

Collapsing the scrum: There are several ways that the props can be penalised during a scrum, but this is the most common. Scrummaging is often referred to as 'the dark arts', as it is hard to see what's going on, and most of it is probably illegal. Ordinarily, a team that gets a good shove on will win a penalty.

Against the head: When a pack wins a scrum off the opposition put-in. Big bragging points.

Lineout calls: The code used to tell your team where the ball will be thrown. If the opposition guesses right, then they might *steal the lineout*.

Penalty try: When the referee deems that a side would have scored, had the opposition not deliberately fouled to stop them. Usually the result of numerous penalties for collapsing the scrum or pulling down a maul.

Shot at goal: If it's in range, a penalty can result in three points, when the kicker boots the ball between the uprights. Anywhere in the opposition half is in range for top kickers.

Drop-goal: Another three pointer – when a player kicks the ball over the crossbar on the half-volley in open play. If the commentator says the fly half has 'gone *back to the pocket*', the player's about to attempt a drop goal.

Charge down: The opposition can attempt to charge down a punt, drop goal or conversion, by putting their arms, face or body in the way. A charge-down doesn't count as a knock-on, so the player can pick up the ball or score a try if it ricochets over the try line.

Dummy: When a player feints to pass or kick a ball, but then doesn't. The defender will either buy the dummy or ignore it (and then smash him).

Pushover Try: When a pack of forwards drives the opposition scrum backwards and over the try line, so the number eight dots down.

Sin bin: For repeat penalties, dangerous play or a professional foul, a player can 'see yellow'. They get ten minutes in the sin-bin for a yellow card, giving the opposition a one-man advantage. A 'straight red' offence – earning a red card and early bath – is usually for dangerous or violent play.

Grubber: To kick the ball so that it bounces forward along the ground.

Inside his 22: The rugby pitch has lots of lines, but two of the most important are the 22-yard lines, which are 22 yards from both teams' try lines. The area of grass between try line and 22-yard line is called *the 22*. Players inside their 22 can kick the ball out on the full (without bouncing it first) unless they are thrown the ball across the 22-yard line. If they catch a kick in their 22 before it bounces, they can call a mark (by shouting 'mark!' very loudly) and they gain a free kick. When teams *camp inside your 22*, they are repeatedly attacking.

22 drop-out: When the ball is kicked over the try line by the attacking side, a defender can touch the ball down or kick it dead. His team then gets a drop-out (a restart with a drop kick) on the 22-yard line. If he 'carries it over' himself, and is forced to touch down, then the attacking side gets a *scrum five* (five yards from the try line).

Truck and Trailer: A quirky rule, which results in a penalty. If a maul breaks off and then travels forward, the player in front of the ball carrier is not allowed to impede a would-be tackler. It is a form of *crossing*, when you are deemed to be obstructing the tackler. Blocking is OK in American Football, but not rugby.

Use it!: Short for 'use it or lose it'. The ref will tell the scrum-half that he has three seconds to pass the ball after it emerges from the back of a ruck or maul. Previously, a team could run down the clock, looking for options.

Hospital pass: To throw the ball to a static teammate who becomes a sitting duck for a big hit.

Going upstairs: When the referee isn't sure about the grounding for a try – or he thinks there might be foul play – he will confer with the *Television Match Official (TMO)* – who will look at the replays from multiple angles.

Touch rugby: Non-contact rugby, where you touch or tag the ball carrier. Good for fitness and basic skills like passing, catching, finding space and running. An excellent way to introduce new players to rugby.

RUGBY LEAGUE

RUGBY LEAGUE split away from Rugby Union at the end of the 19th Century, for geographical and ideological reasons. Money too – the stuffy Southerners refused to recompense elite players, while the gritty Northerners thought that was unfair. The two 'codes' have bickered ever since.

Throughout their history, the breakaway League has innovated to make their version more spectator friendly, as the clubs needed bums on seats to pay their squads. So, 13 players a side frees up more space to run. They did away with line-outs, rucks and mauls, which are so time-consuming and technically complicated in Union. Six-man scrums became uncontested, giving the flair players more paddock to strut their stuff.

The distinctive system of *play-the-ball* restarts (the tackled player rolls the ball backwards through his legs to a teammate) keeps the ball in play more. With a set of just six tackles, before possession hands over, there's a higher premium on the basics of rugby (running, passing, tackling, catching, communicating) leading to professionals who are fitter, stronger, faster, tougher and better ball players. There are other key differences: a try is worth four points, not five, although conversions are also two points. Penalty kicks are worth two, not three. Drop goals are one point, not three.

Fans of League will tell you it's a far more exciting sport, easier to watch and has better players. For many northern English towns and great swathes of Australia, it is the only code and a lifelong religion. Union supporters believe League lacks variety and sophistication, although they go green at the gills at the thought of ever having to play full-contact League, because it's so much more physically demanding. Touch rugby is basically non-contact Rugby League.

Talk a good game

Tackle: The team in possession has six tackles in a set, in which they aim to drive down the pitch and ultimately score a try. When a player is put on the ground, that counts as one tackle. The ref will keep count. The tackled player then gets up as quickly as possible (or as quickly as the opposition legally allows him), to keep momentum building and stop the defensive line from organising.

Offside: After the tackle is made, the defensive line must be back 10 yards before the next attack. They're offside if they don't get back. The fans are quick to remind the ref to 'gerremback!'

Heel: The act of stepping over in the play-the-ball, after being tackled.

Hand Over: If the team is tackled in possession six times, they give the ball to the opposition. Usually, the *sixth tackle* or *last tackle* is kicked to gain a better field position or set up a try if close to the line. If they decide to run the ball instead, it's called a *powerplay* and can lead to an immediate hand over.

Dummy half: The player who makes the next move after the play-the-ball. Also called the *acting half back*.

Man of Steel: Rugby League prides itself – with some justification – on being a hard man's sport. This title is given to the best player in the Super League (the premier European league).

Kick and Clap: Pejorative name for Rugby Union, i.e. the players spend most of the time kicking the ball and the spectators applaud every pointless kick.

Hooker: The number nine, who does a lot of the passing and playmaking.

Grapple Tackle: Tackling a player isn't enough – you want to slow him down too, allowing your teammates to line up for the next tackle. Wrapping him up for a split second in a grapple tackle does exactly that.

Crusher tackle: Getting your arm round the ball carrier's neck and pushing his chin into his chest. Painful and slows him down.

'Man of Steel'

Chicken wing: Twisting the ball carrier's arm behind his back on the ground. Illegal, but mightily effective if you get away with it.

Blood bin: Where you're sent to clean up if the claret flows.

Bomb: A high kick for chasing.

Surrender! What the referee calls if he thinks the ball carrier has dived to the ground before being properly tackled. He'll do it so that he can fall in a way that allows him to get the ball away quicker. Defenders are therefore given carte blanche to hold onto him a bit longer on the ground.

Scrum: These are uncontested in League, with six players leaning against six, so the team feeding always wins. The idea is to tie in players, giving the backs more space to attack. Most commonly awarded for knock-ons and forward passes. Forwards do tend to be bigger than backs, but that's so they can do crash balls and big tackles, not scrummaging.

Drag and Drop: To run a sideways line to drag a defender out of position, before dropping a pass to a teammate coming the other way.

Upright Tackle: When the ball carrier is effectively stopped, but not brought to the ground. Avoids extended wrestling.

40/20 rule: Quirky rule, more akin to Real Tennis than rugby. If you're standing within 40 yards of your own line and you kick the ball into touch, on the bounce, within 20 yards of your opponents' try line, then you get the feed at the scrum.

Ball and all: To tackle someone in a way that prevents them from offloading.

Biff: Fighting.

Cannonball: Illegal and dangerous tackle, when you smash into the legs of the ball carrier when he's held standing by teammates.

Flop: To jump on the tackled ball carrier and slow him from getting back up. Illegal, but not always picked up.

Crash ball: To pass the ball to a big lad coming at top speed. Aussies call it a *hit-up*.

RUGBY LEAGUE

See you later: Slang for a hand-off.

Sin bin: Where the naughty boys are sent for 10 minutes.

Goal line drop: If you catch or pick up the ball in your own in-goal area, and get tackled before crossing your own try line, then you must take a drop-kick from beneath the posts, so giving possession back. It leads to an ironic situation where the attacking side is trying to defend their opposition's try line.

CRICKET

ONE OF THE (MANY) JOYS OF CRICKET is that it can be enjoyed on a different number of levels. If you can't place your silly mid-off from your third man, or spot a yorker from a zooter, then you can still have a grand day out. It is the perfect background sport, whether reading the newspaper beyond the boundary rope or keeping half an ear on Test Match Special at work. You don't even need to know that much about what's going on to enjoy the hubbub of a test match or the excitement of a Twenty20 slog-out. One side is batting, the other is bowling, and they'll swap over sooner or later. Whichever does both better usually scores more runs, and therefore wins the match. In two-innings test matches – still viewed as the pinnacle of the sport – honours are even if neither team wins inside five days.

Cricket has evolved rapidly in the last ten years, as batsmen now have the pitches, bats, confidence and licence to score at a much higher rate. The best bowlers still take wickets, but many get punished like never before. As a result, cricket is now much more spectator friendly, with pulsating limited-over matches (T20 and one-dayers) and fast-moving test matches.

There are lots of complicated laws and quirky language, but they shouldn't prove alienating if you stick at it. One way to understand the game is to interpret the action from the perspective of the key protagonists – batsmen, bowlers, captains, fielders and umpires.

The batsman has two main considerations: A) staying in (survive) and B) scoring runs (accumulate). Depending on the state of the game, the pitch, the strength of the bowlers, and his own ability and mindset: defence or attack will be more of a priority at any given time. Although the longer he does A, the easier B becomes. Modern batsmen look to score, then defend if it's a good ball. In the old days, batsmen would defend, waiting to score off a bad ball.

The bowler also has two motivations: C) get the batsmen out (strike) and D) limit the runs they score (contain). Again, the priority will depend on the match situation, the pitch, and the ability and mindset of both himself and the batsmen. Often, the more a bowler does C, the more likely he is to achieve D. The captain will likewise base his strategy – setting the field and choosing the bowler – on the need to take wickets or stop runs, or a combination of the two if the match is in the balance. For the fielders, anticipating whether the batsman is intent on attack or defence is important.

Umpires, who are still crucially important to the smooth running of a match, despite technological advances, shouldn't be swayed by A, B, C, D or any other letter, but make a call on what they see. If available, the Third Umpire will overturn incorrect decisions.

For cricket tragics, there's no need to recommend the game's charms. For those who find it all a bit boring, weird or cliquey, then do please give it another go. If you choose to jump down cricket's rabbit hole, then you'll enter a wonderful land that draws you deeper with every match. The role of each fielder, the pressure on the batsmen, the plan of the bowler, the changing condition of the weather, pitch and ball: they all come into sharp definition. Cricket is certainly complicated, but once you immerse yourself in the culture, you join a rich and fascinating conversation.

Talk a good game

Over: The six balls delivered in a set by a bowler from one end. The next over is from the other end by a different bowler.

Wicket: Either describes the stumps, the pitch, the batsman's 'life', or the act of getting a batsman out.

Maiden: When no runs are scored off an over. A *wicket maiden* is an over where the bowler dismisses a batsman and no runs are scored.

Four: When the ball is hit to the boundary, and bounces at least once on the way.

Six: When the ball clears the boundary.

Offside: Any part of the pitch to the right-hand side of a right-handed batsman. It's the left-hand side to a left-handed batsman. An *off drive* goes into the offside, while the *off stump* is the furthest to the left, as the umpire sees it.

Legside: The opposite. It's also called the *onside* too, just to complicate things.

Run out: A bit like rounders or baseball, when you don't make your ground in time.

Stumped: When the batsman leaves his crease and the wicket-keeper whips off the bails before he gets his foot back behind the line. The *line belongs to the keeper*, in that some part of the boot, bat or body must be behind the line, not just on it. The bowler is credited with the wicket, as long as the batsman isn't attempting to score a run (in which case it's a run out and deemed a *team wicket*).

Leg-before-wicket (lbw): You can be adjudged lbw if the umpire thinks the ball hit your pads in line with the stumps and would have bowled you. He also thinks you didn't hit the ball with your bat and attempted to play a shot. If he thinks the ball pitched outside the leg stump, then he won't give it out, even if it's going to *clean you up*. The law has evolved to stop negative play by batsmen.

Umpire's call: Batsmen and bowlers can refer certain decisions to the *Third Umpire*, who will use television replays and various gadgets to see if his mates on the field got it right. The technology isn't 100 per cent accurate, so for tight calls – where the ball is grazing the stumps or a snick on the bat is inconclusive – the decision stays on the field and is deemed umpire's call. The batsman is still in or out.

Mode of dismissal: Batsmen are primarily bowled, caught, run out, lbw and stumped. Occasionally they hit their own wickets with their bat or body. In practice matches, batsmen often *retire out* to give someone else a chance. They are almost never given for obstructing the field, handling the ball, hitting the ball twice or timed out for taking more than three minutes to walk to the middle.

Declaration: In tests and first class matches, teams get two innings, which are added together. The match must be finished in five or four days respectively, otherwise it's a draw. So a captain may decide to declare a team innings complete, to get the opposition in and push for victory. Some declarations are more courageous than others, as many captains would rather draw than risk losing.

Duck: When the batsman scores no runs – originally because the zero in the scorebook looked like a duck egg. A *golden duck* is first ball. A *ruby duck* is run out without facing a ball, while a *diamond duck* is dismissed on the first ball of the innings.

Pair: As in 'pair of spectacles' i.e. 0–0 meaning to bag two ducks in the same match.

King Pair: To get a golden duck in both innings.

Nightwatchman: A tailender who is promoted up the order to protect the better batsmen at the end of a day.

Show The Maker's Name: To bat stoutly with a straight blade.

Cow Corner: Originally a section of the outfield where *orthodox* or *textbook* batsmen rarely hit the ball, so it was a safe place for cows to graze. With today's more agricultural styles, the term seems even more apt. The bowler (or batsmen's teammates) may shout 'mooo' to pull the slogger's leg.

Agricultural: The opposite of a *textbook stroke,* this is usually a cross-batted hoik, swipe, slog or mow, in the direction of cow corner.

Flat Track Bully: A batsman who is devastating on an easy pitch, but goes missing when the ball is spinning, seaming or hooping about. Often big in stature, they plant their front foot and biff the bowlers to all parts.

Carry your bat: Rare feat in which an opening batsman walks off undefeated, after all his ten mates are dismissed.

Devil's Number: Australian term for 87, their team's bogey number. Often believed unlucky as it is 13 shy of a century, but it was actually a personal fixation of legendary all-rounder Keith Millar that passed into common use.

Nelson: When the score is 111, 222, 333, etc. – considered unlucky by English players. A triple Nelson is 333. Named after Admiral Horatio Nelson and made famous by umpire David Shepherd, who used to hop on one leg to ward off superstition.

Charge: To use your feet and move down the wicket towards the bowler, usually a spinner but also a quicker bowler when the batsman is feeling brave or cocky. If the bowler sees the batsman coming, he might change his length or spear the ball down the legside to get the batsman stumped.

Downtown: taking a bowler Downtown means walloping him back over his head for six.

Gun: A top batsman. A *hack* is the old phrase for a poor one.

Rabbit: A tailender with limited ability. With modern training, there tend to be rather fewer true rabbits nowadays. Also called a *walking wicket*.

Ferret: Goes in after the rabbits. Can barely hold a bat. Commentators often joke that he is followed by the roller, as a quick demise is inevitable.

Bunny: A batsman who always gets out to the same bowler. He is the bowler's bunny. The bowler *has the mockers* or *a hoodoo* on him.

Hutch: Alternative name for the pavilion, especially if it is full of rabbits.

Jack: The number 11 batsman. As in nine, ten, jack or *jackrabbit*. Take your pick.

Anchor: Top order batsman who bats for a long period and holds the team innings together. He is said to *bat through* or *provide the glue*, while others play round him or take risks. Also a verb: *to anchor* (or *sheet anchor*) the innings.

Stonewall: To defend obdurately. Stonewallers are also known as *limpets*. If a team shuts up shop and bats for a draw, then a match turns into a blockathon (which is less boring than it sounds!).

Bottom hand: Classic strokeplay is led by the top hand on the bat, as it aids straight hitting and getting over the ball. Shots led by the bottom hand are more likely to be cross-batted, aerial and less aesthetic. However, in the modern T20 era, the bottom hand is vital for lofting sixes and working the ball into the onside.

Century: To score 100 runs. Also known as *a ton* or *ton-up*. A decent knock whatever the circumstances.

Half-century: 50 runs. On a good pitch, for top-order batsmen, this is seen as par, while it is a fine achievement for a lower-order batsman.

Farm the strike: To score in a way that means you face most of the bowling. Usually means scoring a single (or three) on the fifth or sixth ball of the over. It's either a selfless act to protect a lesser batsman or a selfish one to boost your own score/ importance. Also *shepherd the strike*.

Fishing: Aiming a waft or flashing a drive at a wide delivery outside the off stump. Also, *hanging the bat out* or *having a nibble*. Usually accompanied by choruses of derision from the keeper and slips, who are waiting to catch the edge, nick, snick, tickle or feather.

Gardening: To prod at the pitch in between balls, ostensibly to flatten out bumps or marks from the last ball, which could cause the next to misbehave. In reality, on today's excellent pitches, it makes little difference to the surface, but gardening can help the batsman maintain focus, look like he's in control, disrupt the bowler, avoid eye contact from close fielders, or present an excuse for why he missed the ball.

Corridor of uncertainty: A good length delivery on or just outside the off-stump, which leaves the batsmen in two minds whether to play or leave, especially if the ball is moving. Also: bowling a fourth stump line or keeping the slips interested.

Leave: When the batsman offers no shot, allowing the ball to travel through to the keeper, or to hit his pads (or the stumps if he has misjudged it). It sounds negative, but a 'good leave' is a skilful and even elegant stroke, and a source of frustration for the bowler when he has bowled a peach. Also called *to shoulder arms*.

Periscope: When the batsman ducks a bouncer, but leaves his bat in the air. If the ball strikes his periscope, then he can be caught or score runs, depending on his luck.

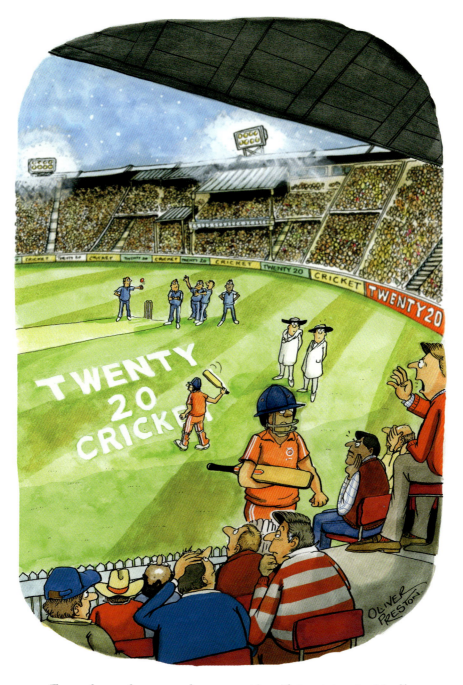

'For goodness sakes, can we have an umpire with twenty-twenty vision?'

CRICKET

Peach: An excellent delivery, which often gets the batsman out. Also known as a *purler, beauty* (or *beaut*), *corker, good nut* or *cherry* (or *seed* if you're an Aussie) and *wicket ball*. An unplayable peach is a *jaffa*.

Hector: Rhyming slang for an abdominal protector (or box).

Nervous nineties: When the batsman closes in on a century and gets jittery. The fielders close in too, while the batsman at the other end gets ready to run like the clappers or shout 'No!' very quickly.

Nurdle: To score runs at a good pace, but with well-placed glances, prods, tucks and taps, rather than biffing the ball. Also called *milking the bowler* (which might need some explanation to the uninitiated).

Pongo: Used more in England, but any onslaught of runs. Also: *giving it some humpty* or *run pie*.

Sawn off: To be given out incorrectly by an umpire. There's an implication that the umpire has rather enjoyed seeing the back of you. Also *triggered*.

Switch hit: When a right-handed batsman reverses his stance and swaps his grip, so he is effectively batting like a left-hander (or vice versa). If done well, you take advantage of the field, confuse the bowler and delight the crowd. If you get out, then you deserve the bowler's well-articulated send-off.

Tail: The lower order batsmen. It usually starts at number eight, but some teams bat deeper. Against weaker teams, the cry 'we're into the tail, lads!' arrives earlier to insult the incoming batsman. If the *tail wags*, the lower order has managed to score heavily or hang about, which doesn't half annoy the opposition.

Stranded: When the not-out batsman is close to a landmark, like a century. Made worse if his captain declares…

Boot Hill: Another term for *Short Leg*, who stands dangerously close to the batsman. Usually a newcomer or the youngest player. So-named after the gunslinger graveyards in the Wild West.

Sledging: To insult the batsman or disrupt his concentration verbally. Also *to chirp*. Originally an Australian term shortened from subtle as a sledgehammer. Some is good-humoured, plenty isn't.

What's in a name?

When travelling, it pays to learn some of the local vernacular. For example, if you're dozing at the side of an oval in Australia and someone shouts: 'Watch out, mate. Dorothy, incoming!' then you should duck. The batsman has just hit a sixer into the bleachers. The term is a rhyming nod to the American columnist and agony aunt Dorothy Dix, arguably the world's most popular journalist in the 20s, 30s and 40s, with a global audience of 60 million. By the end, for entertainment purposes, she was believed to have embellished (faked) the questions she received, something today's columnists would never do… In the Australian parliament, a Dorothy-Dixer is an imaginative question from a backbencher to make the government look good. Dorothy Dixer – sixer!

Dolly: A simple catch. Also, *a sitter*. Possibly derives from an Anglo–Indian term to do with offering food.

Chin music: A barrage of short-pitched bowling, which the batsman needs to fend off his chin. Also called a *throat ball*. It's pinched from American slang – originally to heckle or trash talk – and latterly a baseball term for deliberately pitching the ball at the batter's head.

Perfume ball: To ping the ball past the batsman's nose, so close he can smell the leather. Aussies might say: 'give him a sniff!' A *rib tickler* doesn't get up so high (or the batsman is taller), but is no more enjoyable to play. Also, a *rip snorter*.

Bounced out: When the chin music works, and the batsmen can't cope with the bumpers. He'll get bowled, fend it into the air and edge a hook shot, and so *fall into the trap*.

Badged: Australian term for when a batsman is hit on the helmet by a bumper. Brits might say *sconed*.

Crowd catch: When the spectators roar because they think a catch has been taken. In fact, it was a *bump ball* (played straight down into the ground) and so not out.

Drinks Waiter: Euphemism for the twelfth man, who carries the drinks for his teammates, instead of playing. Some fulfil their duties with dignity, others sulk all day.

Coffin: Large rectangular box for carrying the endless list of cricket kit. Some are neat and ordered. Others explode across the dressing room.

Have a blow: To take a rest after a bowling spell. The skipper might say it to a bowler, if he's *gone round the park*.

Silly: In close, as in 'silly mid on' or 'silly point'. The perfect descriptor!

Death rattle: The dreaded noise of the ball hitting the stumps when you're bowled. Also, *to have your furniture rearranged*. Or *Timber!*

Toe crusher: A fast in-swinging *yorker* aimed at the *blockhole* and the batsman's feet. The Aussies call it a *sandshoe crusher*.

Wear the ball: To be hit by the ball. Grittier batsman will prefer to wear the ball, rather than use their bat and risk giving a catch.

Join the Dots: To complete a maiden (or generally bowl economically). In the book, the scorer will join the six dots to form an M. Fielders might encourage the bowler on the last ball of a runless over by saying 'join it with a W'. A wicket maiden is shown as W in the book.

Michelle: When the bowler takes five wickets in an innings. Rhyming slang for a 'five-fer' from movie star Michelle Pfeiffer.

Heavy Ball: Slightly vague term that implies the ball is quicker and hits the bat or keeper's gloves harder than it looks. Good reputation to get.

Plumb: To be hit on the pads, bang in front of the stumps. It should be given out lbw, but it isn't always…

Buffet bowling: Rank bowling, usually with plenty of *half-trackers* (long hops), *full-*

bungers (full tosses) and legside dross, so that the batsman can 'help himself' to some cheap runs. Also called *cafeteria bowling*.

Death overs: The final overs of a limited-overs match. Specialists are good at 'bowling yorkers at the death'.

Part Timer: An occasional bowler, who is brought on when the conditions suit or the other bowlers are jiggered.

Dibbly dobbly: A medium pace bowler who wobbles down a variety of swingers, cutters and slower balls. Sometimes dismissed as *pie throwing* or *Bassets* (as in All Sorts) or *trundling*.

The Yips: When a bowler suffers a confidence crisis and can no longer release the ball at the right time. It might fly over the keeper's head or smash into the ground a few feet away. The first couple of *yippies* are quite funny, but it quickly gets painful to watch.

Picket fence: When a single is scored off every ball of the over – 111111. Also another name for the boundary.

Turn and Bounce: The dream combination for spinners. Every chance of a Michelle.

The condition of the pitch is always cause for debate. As with anything important in cricket, there's some great language to grease the conversation:

Bunsen: A turning pitch, as in Bunsen Burner. Good for spinners.

Sticky Wicket: A wet pitch. The ball skids and stops. Good for seamers.

Sticky Dog: A wet, tacky pitch, drying in the sun. Good for seamers.

Featherbed: A flat pitch that offers nothing to the bowler. Good for batsmen.

Belter: Same as a featherbed. Great for batsmen.

Road: Same as a belter. Also a *street* or *motorway*. Great for batsmen.

Green Top: Lots of grass. Hard work for batsmen. Good news for the quicks.

Dustbowl: A dry pitch, typically in the Sub-Continent. Good for spinners.

Cabbage patch: A luscious, uneven bog. Great for all bowlers.

Minefield: An uneven pitch, where the ball can pop and jump. Good for quicks.

Wearing wicket: An old pitch with deep footmarks and cracks. Good for spinners.

AMERICAN FOOTBALL

THE WINNING TEAM SCORES THE MOST POINTS from touchdowns and field goals. The aim of the game is to advance the ball downfield as a team, either running with the ball in hand until tackled or throwing it to a buddy. If you can carry the ball or pass to a receiver inside your opponent's end zone, then you score a touchdown (albeit you don't actually need to touch the ball down on the ground, like in rugby).

Touchdowns can be scored from anywhere, but most come from short range. The team in possession will progress through a series of downs, with four chances (downs) to move the ball forward ten yards (which is why the pitch is painted in yardage lines). Make your ten yards, and you get another four downs, creeping ever closer to the end zone. If the defensive team successfully stop you from gaining ten yards, then they get the ball, although the offensive team will usually punt the ball downfield or attempt a field goal on the fourth down to gain a better field position.

Teams have eleven players on the field, although squads number 45 to allow specialist offense or defence players. For example, you don't want your kicker or quarterback making tackles all night. On this side of the pond, we often look snootily at the bells and whistles, machismo and exuberance, nachos and cheerleaders, time-outs and half-time shows. The fact we call it *gridiron* immediately makes it sound drabber. But American Football is a wonderful spectacle, filled with extraordinary athleticism, strategy and teamwork. Watching it is time well spent.

Talk a good game

Plays: Carefully-orchestrated strategies, called by the head coach or quarterback, that involve all eleven players blocking opponents or trying to get in space, with the goal of moving the ball downfield.

Touchdown: When a team carries the opposition's goal line with the ball, or completes a pass to a receiver in the end zone. Worth six points.

Field goal: Usually attempted on the fourth down, if the kicker is in range to place kick the ball through the uprights. Worth three points.

Extra point: Similar to a conversion in rugby, teams gain an extra point by kicking the ball through the uprights after scoring a touchdown. Usually a formality, and only worth one point. If the team needs two points, often a last throw of the dice at the end of the match, then they can try to take the ball into the end zone again, although it seldom works.

Safety: This one gets the defensive team whooping and bashing helmets. When a member of the offensive team is tackled in his own end zone. Worth two points, but also very rare.

Quarterback: The playmaker, who is often the team's figurehead. In high school movies, he dates the prom queen. His job is to pass the ball to receivers, either by handing or throwing. Has the option to run too, although he then risks being sacked and roughed up.

The snap: When the centre, who stands in the middle of the offensive line, flicks the ball back between his legs to the quarterback (similar to rugby league's play-the-ball).

Running back: Another marquee player, with the speed, strength and agility to run the ball forward, often through a mass of players trying to hammer him.

Linebacker: A key player in defence. Often a free agent who runs behind the line, picking off runners or rushing the passer.

Muff: To drop or mishandle a loose ball.

The defence: The wrecking squad who aim to stop the opposition by tackling, intercepting passes or causing fumbles.

Sack: To tackle the quarterback before he has thrown the ball. Cue much excitement and strutting from whoever did it.

Fumble: When the ball is knocked from the carrier's hands. Both teams can then play it, so it may cause a turnover of possession. The expression 'to drop the ball' came from American Football.

Interception: When the defence cleanly catch a pass meant for a receiver. They then have possession, and will try to advance as far as possible before being tackled.

Incomplete: When the receiver fails to catch the ball cleanly, or is legally impeded from doing so.

Special teams: Usually for kicking plays, such as punts, field goals and extra point attempts. The offence will have specialist kickers, while the defence have specialist blockers and returners.

Backward pass: Most passes go forward, but a team can pass back as often as they like on a play. Rugby players will wonder why they don't do it more often.

Black Monday: The day after the end of the season, when unsuccessful coaches get called in for a chat.

Line of scrimmage: The line on which the offence and defence must stand prior to each *down*. Almost, but not quite touching each other.

Block: Impeding your opponent from getting to where they want to be. The successful quarterback relies on good blocking. The term *block and tackle* is often used to describe the need to get back to basics in business.

Camp fodder: Derogatory term for players who make the training camp, but have no chance of playing during the season.

OLIVER PRESTON.

Drive: When the team combines a number of first downs and sets up a good scoring chance.

Flag: A weighted yellow cloth thrown by a field official to indicate that a foul has been committed. The coach can throw a red cloth to challenge a call.

Gunslinger: A gung-ho quarterback with the arm to throw long.

Hail Mary: When the quarterback throws into a group of players in the end zone, hoping one of his team will catch it.

Huddle: When the brains trust gets together to discuss the next play.

Juke: To dodge or sidestep a tackler.

NFL: National Football League. The top of the game in the US.

Pump fake: When the quarterback fakes to pass the ball.

Rush: Either an attempt to tackle or hurry an opponent, or a running play, usually by a running back.

Scoop and score: A fumble recovered by the defence that results in a touchdown.

Slobber-knocker: A big hit.

Stiff-arm: To push off a tackler. A *hand-off* in rugby.

Hand-off: The act of giving the ball to another player, usually from the quarterback to a running back.

Three-and-out: When an offensive team fails to make a new first down in three attempts, and so is forced to punt on the fourth.

Throwaway: When the quarterback deliberately throws the ball out of bounds. He's about to be sacked and has nobody open, so gets rid of the ball to avoid losing yardage or making a fumble.

Wide receiver: Fast and springy, these catchers make some of the most spectacular plays, snaffling the ball high above the ground in the end zone. Some are the best dancers too.

Monday morning quarterback: A pundit or fan who makes all the right calls and moves with the benefit of hindsight in their newspaper column or by the office watercooler.

Zebra: Friendly term for the officials, who wear black and white stripes.

Backfield: The group of offensive players – the running backs and quarterback – who line up behind the line of scrimmage.

Super Bowl: The championship match of the season, and one of the biggest sporting fixtures on the planet. Played on the first Sunday in February – Super Sunday – the two conference winners slug it out for glory. Now as famous for the half-time show and adverts, as the action itself.

Return: To run a kick back – some of the most dramatic touchdowns are scored from punt returns from speedsters with good footwork – like a wide receiver or running back. If it's not on, or the catcher doesn't want to risk a fumble, he can gesture for a *fair catch* (like a *mark* in rugby) or let the ball bounce, and it's a first down from where it stops.

Audible: A last-second change from the play already decided upon in the huddle. The quarterback shouts in code to change the play once he and his teammates are at the line of scrimmage. Usually occurs when the quarterback sees something in the opposing defence, which means the original play called would not be successful.

Bomb: To make a long pass.

Chain gang: A group of men with a ten-yard rope who assist the officials.

Completion: A forward pass that is successfully caught by an eligible receiver.

Draft: The annual horse-trading in which the leading college players are selected by the NFL teams. The team that finished bottom gets first pick. If a last pick player comes good, then he's *a steal*.

Locker room: The dressing room. Often huge. The press are usually allowed in the locker room afterwards.

Playbook: The coach's secret plans and strategies. Players are supposed to know it inside out.

Roughing the passer: A slap on the wrists (15 yard penalty) if someone hammers the quarterback after he has thrown the ball.

Spike: To throw the ball into the turf after scoring a touchdown. May spark an intricate dance that will go viral on YouTube the next day.

Time out: A team gets three short breaks every half to think or rethink their next moves.

BASKETBALL

PART OF THE JOY OF BASKETBALL IS ITS SIMPLICITY. Both teams try to put the ball in the basket, and stop the opposition from doing so. You get two points for a basket and three points if it's thrown from beyond the *three point line* (a semicircle around the basket). Fouls result in two free throws, which score you two points if you get the first, then one point for the second. The team with the most points at the end is the winner.

Yet, basketball is about much more than giants bouncing balls and shooting hoops. It may have its grandstand players, but basketball is a slick team sport, which marries different physical attributes, roles, sizes and skills.

Understanding the five playing positions gives a clear insight into how the game works:

Point Guard (PG): Often much shorter than the others, this guy sets the tempo and starts off most of the offensive plays, taking the ball upcourt when his team have regained possession. If one of the big fellas steals the ball at the net, then he'll usually ping it straight to the point guard, before lumbering forward himself. The PG is a brilliant passer and handler, pulling the strings. Quick enough to take the ball to the basket, and accurate enough to nail three-pointers. The best can boss the game without ever scoring. Immensely fit, he's the heartbeat of the team.

Shooting Guard (SG): A size up from the point guard, he's a long range shooting pro. Also known as the *two guard*, he'll move in on *screens* set by taller teammates, ready to shoot, pass to another, or drive to the basket. Coming in with pace behind the shot, he can grab offensive rebounds. Will do a lot of the dirty work. Sometimes known as the *garbage man*, because he cleans up after everyone else.

Small Forward (SF): Usually not that small… In fact, the *three-man* needs to be tall enough to compete with the giants, but also with the agility and handling ability of a point guard. And he can shoot too, from anywhere. At one end, he'll be acing layups and dunks, then seconds later blocking shots, stealing and rebounding down the other. The very best are true all-rounders: high octane showmen and worth every cent to their franchise.

Power Forward (PF): These are the enforcers and tough guys, who can bully the opposition into submission. The number four needs to mix it at the sharp end and muscle his way to the hoop, so he can probably benchpress more than the others and is happy to let them know. Great hands and agility for a big man, he needs to catch quick passes and score his share on the baseline. He can slug it out on the rebounds, but move with speed further out. For all the machismo, the best also bring a silky bag of tricks. If someone ends up on the deck, there's a good chance the grinning power forward has put him there.

Centre (C): The tallest of the tall, with some well over the seven foot mark. While dropping the ball into the basket is one of his jobs, the centre also sets up the plays for others, posting the ball with his back to the basket, or laying up dunks. Will use his height to block and grab rebounds, putting away offensive rebounds with ease. A good centre is a points machine at one end, and a brick wall at the other, quickly putting your team in control. If these *Franchise Players* are on song, there's not a whole lot you can do to stop them.

Talk a good game

Alley-oop: A real crowd pleaser, when one player lobs the ball up for another to dunk it.

Brick: A duff shot that ends up clanking off the rim.

Free throw line: Where the free throws are taken from. Also known as the *charity stripe*.

Downtown: To score from a long way away.

Hack: A foul, usually resulting in a free throw.

Take it to the hole: To drive in at the basket, and score.

OLIVER PRESTON.

In the paint: Inside the free throw line, i.e. close to the basket.

Rock: Another name for the ball.

Technical foul: If you bash into another player, then that's a *personal foul*, and it happens all the time. A *T* or technical foul arrives from a non-contact infraction such as swearing at an official or faking a foul. Two in a match and you're out of there.

Three-pointer: A field goal from behind the three point line. Also called a *trey*.

Travelling: To move forward three steps without bouncing the ball. Results in a foul and turnover. Also called *walking*.

All Day: When somebody never misses, they'll 'make the shot all day'.

And One: If the player gets fouled when shooting, but still scores, then they get an extra free throw to make it a three point play. If he's attempting a three-pointer, then he can get a four point play.

Baby Hook: Nothing babyish about it. A variation of a *sky hook,* when a player makes a wide, one-handed arcing shot that's hard to block. Made famous by Magic Johnson at the LA Lakers.

Black Hole: Derogatory term for a player who never passes, but goes for the basket himself every time.

Break Ankles: When a player is made to fall over, either with a nudge or fancy footwork.

Bringing the House Down: A player on a hot shooting streak.

Three second violation: Players can only loiter in the key (the area beneath the basket) for three seconds. Any longer is a foul. Also called camping in the key. Think 'goal hanging' in football.

Bucket: Another name for the basket, or scoring a basket. Also a term for someone who is scoring a lot.

Bury a jumper: A term of praise for someone who has made a lovely jump shot.

Crunch Time: When the scores are close and the clock is ticking down at the end of the match. The *money player* will *deliver in the clutch* and nail a *dagger* to win the game.

Dropping Dimes: Spinning pin-perfect passes for others to score.

Facial: To slap the ball in an opponent's face while shooting.

Fadeaway: To shoot when leaning away from the basket, often losing balance.
Find the Open Man: Pass to a mate in the clear.

Floater in the Key: An arcing shot, taken from close to the bucket. Also known as a *teardrop*.

Fouling Strategy: To deliberately foul players who are weak at free throws, so you get the ball back.

Gym Rat: Someone who spends all their spare time shooting hoops in the gym.

He Got Game: An all-rounder.

Kill the Clock: To use all of the allotted 24 seconds before taking a shot, with a view to closing out the match.

Monster Jam: A seismic dunk.

Nailed to the Bench: Unfortunate term for someone who rarely gets on the court. Also *picking up splinters, pine time* or *riding the pine*.

Over the Limit: A team can only make five fouls in a quarter before the opposition get two free throws. A player can only make five in the match – a sixth sees him sidelined.

Pound the Boards: To tussle for rebounds under the basket.

Ride Him While He's Hot: To get the ball to a player on a hot streak.

Soft on D: Good at going forward, but weak in defence.

Hops: Someone with spring. Often describes the (comparatively) shorter Point Guard who can't just drop it in the basket.

Squeeze the Ball: To regain control of the ball on a rebound.

Taken to School: To be consistently bettered by another player. A torrid experience for the pupil.

Dialling long distance: To take a three point throw

Windmill: A wide-arcing dunk.

GOLF

IN STROKEPLAY TOURNAMENTS (such as The Open or The Masters), the winner takes the fewest shots over four rounds of 18 holes. If there's a tie, then the champion is decided in a play-off. In matchplay tournaments (most famously The Ryder Cup), the player or team that wins the most number of holes is the winner.

The course is set up to test the golfer's ability to hit the ball in many different ways, from 300-yard drives off the tee to three-foot putts on the greens. Different courses suit different styles – big hitters, accurate approach play or a solid short-game (chipping and putting) – while the local weather conditions play their part. But most golf is decided between the ears. It's the players who can hold their nerve under extreme pressure who end up regular champions (and fabulously wealthy). The old cliché: 'drive for show, put for dough' rings as true as 'catches win matches' in cricket. Ultimately, golfers need to get the ball in the hole and that can be blessed difficult when you're six feet away from winning something you've dreamt about all your life.

Talk a good game:

The Majors: The four most prestigious strokeplay tournaments – The Masters, The US Open, The Open and the PGA Championship. To be a 'Major-winner' is one of the greatest accolades in golf. Only a handful of players have won all four, known as a Career Grand Slam.

The Green Jacket: The 'trophy' for the winner of The Masters, played at Augusta National in Georgia every year. The previous winner puts the jacket on the new champion in an awkward ceremony in the Butler Cabin, thereby making him an honorary member of the course. It's all very kitsch, but every pro dreams of it.

'Since I retired, the wife really looks forward to some quality golf with me.'

The Claret Jug: The trophy for The Open (usually referred to as The British Open) dates back to 1873. The winner holds it aloft, then takes away a medal. If he wins it three times, he gets a replica. Up until 1929, the winner had the cost of the medal taken out of the prize money.

The Ryder Cup: A biennial team matchplay competition over three days, between Europe and the United States. Named after businessman Samuel Ryder, who sponsored the event in the 1920s and donated the iconic trophy. Unmissable drama.

Halve: In matchplay, to draw a hole or the match. The hole or match is halved. Honours even.

Dormie: To be the same number of holes up, as there are left. For example, dormie two is 'two up, two to play'. Therefore, you can't lose, although you can still halve the match or be taken into a play-off. Failing to win from dormie will feel like a loss. Thought to come from the French *dormir* (to sleep), as the golfer can relax, and allegedly introduced by French-speaking Mary Queen of Scots, who played a bit, although the story is likely apocryphal.

Fat: A mistimed shot, where you've hit the ground before the ball, which will either dribble forward or fall short of the intended target. May create a big divot and sore wrists. Also, *to chunk* or *hit thick*, or *chilli dip*.

Shank: A total duff. The ball can shoot off in any direction, although usually into the nearest bush or ditch. Can be a round killer or even lead to the yips.

Stiff: To knock the ball sweetly, often to within just a small putt of the hole. Heart-breaking for your opponent.

Right out of the screws: To make a perfect connection. Dates to the old days when woods were actually made of wood, and attached to the centre of the club by screws.

Casual water: Fancy name for a puddle. It's not intended as a water hazard, so the player can lift and drop without a penalty.

Sandbagger: What's in a name? Not a good reputation to get, this is someone who can play better than they say they can. A sandbagger might claim a higher handicap in a friendly game or talk down their ability beforehand, with a view to hustling their opponent. Rather aptly, the word has an inglorious past. In the 19th Century, street gangs often made cheap weapons by putting sand (and the odd pebble) in a stocking. Sandbagging was smacking your enemy on the noggin. This expression then passed to poker. A player might attempt to mislead their opponents about how good their hand is, by only raising the pot by a little at a time and keeping several players in the game. Only at the end would they reveal their true position – and clobber the others with a flush.

What's in a name?

Golf terminology is perhaps best known for its quirky scoring system. *Par* is the standard for a hole. One stroke over is a *bogey*. Two over is a *double bogey* (or *buzzard*). One stroke under is a *birdie*. Two under is an *eagle*. Three under is an *albatross*. Four under is a *condor*, although you're more likely to see a dodo… The oldest of these is the bogey, which was the original par. When standard scores for holes and courses were introduced, in England in the 19th Century, players were more consumed with beating the course, rather than each other. A certain Major Charles Wellman, playing at Great Yarmouth GC, described the course as a 'regular Bogey Man'. The name passed into popular usage and players said they were 'playing Colonel Bogey' (which duly inspired the military tune). The reason we're not using the same system today is because Americans demoted the bogey to one over par (a stock exchange term). Birdie is another Americanism. They used to say 'bird' as we might say 'peach' or 'beauty', for example, 'that was a bird of a shot'. Therefore, a one-under became a birdie. A big birdie? An eagle. A rare birdie? An albatross. Even bigger than an albatross? The fabled South American condor…

Ace: Another name for a hole-in-one. Costly for amateurs, who are expected to buy the whole clubhouse a drink. More lucrative for pros, who often win a car.

Army Golf: To hit the ball in alternative directions – left, right, left, right – down the fairway.

Back Door: When the ball drops in the opposite side of the cup, having threatened to *lip out*. Cue a big sigh of relief.

Four-jab: Taking four putts to get the ball down. 'Dicky had a putt for birdie on the third, but then four-jabbed. Walked off with a double bogey. He didn't speak again till the fifteenth.'

Fried Egg: When only half the ball is visible in the bunker. Also: *plugged* or *pluggingtons*.

Afraid Of The Dark: An admonishment for a ball that refuses to fall in the hole, often repeatedly.

Monkeys, camels and hippos: A fun scoring system in which you get penalised for going in the trees, bunkers and water. A *gorilla* is out of bounds, while a *snake* is a three-putt.

Beach: Another name for going in a bunker. 'I spent a lot of time on the beach today.' Also: *Kitty litter.*

Big Dog: The driver. Many amateurs will leave the big dog in the bag until the longest drive competition (or they have nothing else to lose).

Handicap: A universal scoring system that allows players of different abilities to have a close match. *Scratch* is to play without any added shots. If you have a handicap of 14, say, then the course par is no longer 72, but 86. A Five Handicapper would need to shoot 77 to match your 86.

Stableford: A handicap points game, where the player gets four points for an eagle, three for a birdie, two for a par and one for a bogey.

Blob: To get no points on a hole, when playing Stableford. You put a fat zero on the scorecard.

Bandit: A golfer who plays markedly better than their official handicap. Not as bad as a sandbagger, as it may not be so devious.

Cabbage: Deep, thick, impenetrable rough. Also known as *spinach*.

Banana Ball: A fade (or more likely a slice) that swings off to the right (of a right-handed golfer).

Dance floor: The green. Also known as the *carpet*.

Chicken Stick: A go-to club when faced with a tough shot that you don't want to risk muffing up. 'Rather than blast a three wood off a dodgy lie, he chicken-sticked his six iron.'

Duck Hook: A horrible hook that spears off left into the cabbage. Also called a *snap hook* or a *Ken Livingstone* (too far left)…

Slice: An exaggerated fade that bananas off to the right. Also known as a *Jean-Marie Le Pen* (too far right)…

Duffer: Another name for a *hacker*. Struggles to get the ball airborne.

Flatstick: Another name for the putter, as it has one flat edge.

Flop shot: A shot played just off the green with an open blade, sending the ball high into the air, so it stops immediately next the hole. Needs a decent backswing, so if the player *thins* (catch the ball with base of the club), it can end up 30 yards away.

Flub: A disastrous shot that can ruin your round. Usually ends up out of bounds or in deep trouble.

Foot Wedge: Euphemism for a cheat who uses his boot to kick the ball into a better position.

Gimme: In matchplay, or friendly golf, when you're not asked to putt out, because the ball is so close to the hole. Some players are generous with their gimmes (especially if they want them in return), others give nothing over two feet. The distance of the putter shaft to the grip – or *in the leather* - is a rough guide for a gimme.

Slow walk: When the nervous putter gives his opponent as much time as possible to give his next putt. If spotted, it will never be given!

Knee-knocker: A short putt that suddenly looks very long and difficult if it's important. Also a *nasty three footer*.

Grow teeth: A plea to the ball to stop quickly, when headed towards a pond or likely to rush past the hole.

Hanging lie: When the ball is above the golfer's feet.

In the jaws: When the ball stops right at the edge of the hole.

OLIVER PRESTON.

Juicy lie: When the ball is sitting up invitingly in the rough. Also, a *kind lie*. Will leave your opponent cursing their luck if you stiff it to four feet.

On a charge: When a golfer is draining birdies and eagles, and moving up the leader board. Also *on fire* and *running hot*. Can send shudders through the rest of the field, especially if it's a grandstand player.

Pin high: When the ball lands on or near the green, dropping at the same distance as the flag. Great distance control.

Jungle: Where the monkeys live. Hitting the ball into the thickest, remotest part of the course.

Kick: A good bounce forward, either down the fairway or onto the green. The player will often cajole the ball saying 'now kick!', although that's often because they know they've under-clubbed it.

Lag: To deliberately leave a shot or putt short, rather than risk running into trouble. The next shot will be easy, and so danger avoided. 'I wish I'd lagged it like Kevin. He got a bogey, while I blobbed.'

Lay up: Similar to lag, but usually used in conjunction with a hazard, like a bunker or pond. Big hitters will attempt to *fly* the hazard.

Lip out: When the ball looks like it's going to fall in the hole, but spins off the rim. Inevitably put down to bad luck, not bad putting.

Lumberjack: A golfer who regularly visits the woods.

Milk the Grip: When the golfer holds the club like he's milking a cow's udder. This constant gripping and re-gripping is often a sign of nerves, but may just be the way they play.

Mouth Wedge: To try gain an advantage by putting off the opponent with sly digs or endless yap. 'Are those clubs too small for you?' is a famous example of *getting inside a player's head*. Pro golfers will learn to blank it out.

Muff: A duff shot.

Mulligan: When the golfer gets to play a muffed shot again. Often, amongst friends, you might get one Mulligan per round. You use it when you choose. Its origin is contested, but neither version is very interesting, save there was some guy called Mulligan… A *Gilligan* is when your opponent can make you retake a very good shot.

Nineteenth Hole: The clubhouse bar, where great feats are retold and great shanks forgotten.

Iffy: General term for something which is a bit dodgy. An 'iffy lie', an 'iffy shot', an 'iffy ball', an 'iffy bloke', etc.

In his bag: To have the ability to play a certain shot. 'Yep, Alec's got the flop shot in his bag.'

'What a coincidence, I'm looking at your file as we speak.'

Nip it: To hit the ball cleanly off the surface, without taking a divot. Useful on a tight lie.

Reload: To play your shot again, usually after hitting the ball out-of-bounds, but also for a Mulligan.

O.B.: Out of bounds. Gone. Also known as *OOB*. Reload!

Aim at the flag: Sounds counter-intuitive, but *pin-seeking* is often fraught with danger, as you'll be in trouble if you miss, even by a whisker. Far safer to aim for the 'pin high in the heart of the green'.

Rainmaker: To hit the ball up to the heavens.

Robbed: When the player feels he has hit a good shot or putt, but gets no reward. Also, an Arthur Scargill (good strike, poor result). Some laugh off the misfortune, others mutter, sulk and throw their clubs.

Up and down: To chip, either from a bunker or off the green, and then sink the putt. Usually to save par.

U-turn: A putt that sling shots round the cup and comes back at you.

Good enough: An average shot which ends in a good enough position. Again, really annoying for opponents. Also called a *son-in-law* (not what you wanted, but he'll do).

Sandy: Short for a *sandy par*. To land in a bunker, but still *save par*.

Short stuff: On the fairway.

Tap in: A putt of a foot or less. Usually results in a gimme in matchplay. In strokeplay, you must *putt out*.

Sticks: Another name for your clubs.

Ugly: A flub or duff.

Short stick: Another name for the putter, because that's what it is.

Snowman: An '8' on the scorecard.

Victory lap: When the putt slides round the hole and eventually drops. Golf is about fine margins!

Waggle: To wiggle the club in your hands, whilst addressing it. For some it's a pre-shot routine, for others it's a nervous tic.

Watery Grave: When you hit the ball into the drink.

Fresh air: To miss the ball completely. Also a *whiff*.

Wormburner: A ball that shoots along the ground.

Yips: When the golfer can't control their hands on the green. Their putter jerks and wobbles like a rubber snake. Three-foot putts look nearer 40 when the yips strike.

An Adolf: Two shots in a bunker.

A Tony Blair: Promised plenty, but too much spin.

CROQUET

FOR ALL ITS PRETENCES AT BEING A GENTEEL GARDEN PARTY GAME, we all know that croquet is a nasty and vindictive pursuit – but in the most enjoyable way! Ganging up on loved ones, and then knocking their ball into a flower bed is deeply embedded in the British psyche. Top class croquet matches are no less malicious, albeit the players can't put their foot on the ball and they won't storm off when they are three hoops behind. Typically, perhaps, there isn't global consensus on the rules of the sport, with several

rival factions, although Association Croquet is arguably the most dominant and brings together the top nations worldwide.

In Association Croquet, the court is largely as you might expect, with three hoops at either end and the stripy *rover* peg in the centre. The big difference from your common or garden croquet is that a player or pair has two balls – either the red and yellow, or the black and blue – which he, she or they must *run* through the six hoops, and then back again, before hitting them against the peg. With a point for each hoop, and one at the end, there are therefore 26 points up for grabs, although points are more important in timed matches. Usually, it's first past the post who wins.

What's in a name?

Does one roquet or croquet?

The answer is both. The aim – a lot like snooker – is to make as big a *break* as possible, with lots of consecutive strokes before the opponent has their go. You get another stroke for *running* (going through) a hoop. Choosing either ball, the player will *roquet* any of the other three balls by knocking theirs against it. He then picks up his ball and places it next to the roqueted ball. The next thwack of the mallet, which will send both balls off at different angles, is the eponymous *croquet* stroke. To repeat, you can't put your foot on your ball. With the *continuation* stroke, the break continues, and the player can either roquet another ball or try to run a hoop.

A player can only roquet each ball once per hoop, but once he has run a hoop, he can roquet them all again. As such, the very best players will get round the whole court in one go. As much fun as it is to play, you probably need to be a proper sports tragic to watch a three-hour game of croquet.

'I'd say that was OUR game.'

Talk a good game

Backward ball: The trailing ball, which has run fewer hoops. The forward ball is, well, further forward.

Break down: A polite way of saying that the player has muffed up and their break is over.

Double tap: A double hit – when there's a clear tack-tack when the mallet strikes the ball. At the discretion of the referee, if the players' ears disagree.

Hoop: The metal upside down U, which can prove so difficult to pass through. Interestingly, the Americans call them *wickets*.

Leave: A bit like a *safety* in snooker, when the player knows his break is over, he can try to leave the balls in as difficult a spot as possible for the opponent who will play next.

Baulk: The imaginary boundary line around the court, where the balls are placed at the start of the game, and where balls smacked off the court are replaced.

Rover ball: When a ball has run all 12 hoops it becomes a rover ball. It can now be pegged out, used to peel your own ball or generally cause a nuisance. But beware, your opponents may use it to their own advantage.

Peg out: To hit a rover ball against the peg, so removing it from the game. Players may want to keep it alive, as it can aid getting the backward ball round.

Peel: To knock another ball through its next hoop. This would usually be your own ball, but in complicated handicap matches, you might knock your opponent's through.

Running the hoop: Going through the hoop. It is deemed to have run if no part of the ball is visible from behind. (So half-way doesn't count…).

Pioneer: To knock one of the other balls towards a distant hoop, to help your break continue. Definitely a sign of confidence.

Push: To make a duff contact with the ball.

Rush: A strong roquet stroke that bashes the roqueted ball to a good position, whether closer to another ball or the next hoop. Of course, if you miss, then you look a bit silly.

Scatter shot: You can only roquet a ball once, but you can whack yours into it again if you so choose. It's the end of your break, but you will hopefully put your opponent's ball into a less risky position.

Tice: A tempter and teaser. To lure your opponent into roqueting – and then missing – your ball, by putting it in a difficult position which is just too enticing to pass up. Sneaky…

Wired: When the wire of the hoops (or the wooden peg) impedes your opponent's ball or strike. As a result, they can't roquet you or themselves. They may choose to lift the ball, and then play it from the baulk, but it's still a very smart 'leave'.

SUMO

THERE'S A HUGE AMOUNT OF TRADITION AND FANFARE that
accompanies sumo wrestling, but essentially it is a very simple concept and is
often concluded within a matter of seconds. Indeed, the name sumo itself –
translated as 'rushing at the same time' – gets to the heart of it. Two wrestlers
(*rikishi*) enter a circular ring (*dohyo*) of packed dirt, wearing only their thick
loincloths (*mawashi*). When the referee (*gyoji*) signals the start of the bout,
the first man to force his opponent out of the ring, or to make his opponent
touch the ground with any part of his body apart from the soles of his feet, is
declared the winner.

Easier said than done, of course, as these enormous but surprisingly agile
supermen use all their cunning and bulk to confound each other. There are
few more ferocious sights in martial arts as these two warriors collide like
elephant seals, their muscles causing the acres of blubber above to ripple
and slap. Grabbing the loincloth and then pushing or twisting is a proven
technique, as is violently barging head-on. Often, it is a case of might is right,
with the lesser contender literally thrown down onto the ringside spectators.

There are some professional sports in which the amateur enthusiast could
just about get by without looking too much of an idiot. Sumo isn't one of
them.

Talk a good game

Tachiai: This is often the decisive moment in the contest – when the two wrestlers
crunch into each other. Power is key, but also courage and technique, which allow
the smaller dogs to have their day. If the initial smash doesn't separate them, then
lengthier grappling, slapping and bumping ensues, which may drain energy for
later bouts in the *basho*.

'Take care Takata. He's just out of nappies.'

Kimarite: There are many ways to win a bout – 82 to be exact – which are known as the kimarite. It could be bashing with the chest, pushing with the arms from behind, tripping over with one hand on the mawashi, etc. The referee will announce the manner of victory after the bout.

Yokozuna: These are the grand champions, and the icons of the sport, who sit at the top of the rankings. Wrestlers must win bouts and tournaments to rise through the six divisions, with only a very small handful ever reaching the position of Yokozuna. Part of sumo's global popularity in recent years is the emergence of rival champions, including those from abroad.

Sekitori: The fighters in the top two divisions – the *juryo* and elite *makuuchi* – who are the professionals in the leading annual basho. Usually made up of young thrusters and gnarled veterans. When a rikishi enters the juryo, he can wear a special topknot, shaped like a ginkgo tree leaf, as well as the ornamental aprons.

Mawashi: The loincloths. For the professionals, they are made of silk and can be over ten metres in length. If it falls off, they forfeit the bout. Opponents will throw each other by grabbing each other's nappy.

Basho: a tournament. 15 days, with the champion winning the biggest majority of their bouts.

Banzuke: The official list of all participating rikishi in a tournament. The running order is usually stage managed to ensure the top seeds decide the tournament at the end.

Chanko-nabe: The famous stew eaten by wrestlers including a mass of fish, chicken, vegetables, noodles and broth. They will eat huge bowlfuls, along with rice and beer, several times a day.

Harit: To slap in the face.

Henka: Nifty footwork to side-step your opponent's charge at the tachiai, with a view to toppling them out.

Hikiwaza: Pulling the other fella down after a henka.

Sitting on ceremony?

Of course, the ceremonial element of sumo is hugely important and provides much of its charm. The sport has its roots in the Shinto religion, specifically related to the rice harvest, as marked by the bales of rice straw around the dohyo. There is a roof (*Yakata*) above the dohyo to recreate a Shinto shrine, while the gyoji dresses like a Shinto priest. One of the great sights is the *dohyo-iri*, at the start of the day's combat, when all the rikishi in their ornamental *kesho-mawashi* aprons line round the ring, with their bums winking at the audience.

Before each bout (*Torikumi*), the wrestlers politely demonstrate their mutual respect in the *Chirichozu* ritual. They sit crouched, look each other in the eye, rub their hands, then clap them once to catch the attention of the gods. They then put their hands out sideways, palms up then down, before resting them on their knees. This shows that they are unarmed, wearing only their mawashi.

The wrestlers will toss salt about the ring to purify the air. They stamp to squash evil spirits, and drink water to cleanse their bodies. Then, resting both fists on the floor like bulldogs, they wait for the cry '*Hakkeyoi*' from the gyoji, before letting all hell loose on each other.

Ceremony is important again, once the bout is decided. The loser needs to pick himself up – or even climb back up from the crowd – and bow to the winner, before leaving the ring again. The winner crouches, and the referee confirms the result and how it was achieved. The victor then responds by making a closed arm gesture to salute the efforts of the loser. Any show of emotion from either warrior is deemed disrespectful (just one more reason why rikishi wouldn't survive in top flight football).

Heya: A sumo stable, where wrestlers *keiko* (train) and live together. There are strict daily routines, traditions and dress codes, with certain stables adopting different schools of thought.

Inashi: Walloping your opponent from the side to make him topple over.

Okuridashi: To spin your opponent round and push them out from behind.

Shikiri-sen: The white lines at the centre of the ring, where the wrestlers stand pre- and post-bout.

Shisho: The stable master.

Shitatenage: A wedgie. Grabbing the other by his mawashi and throwing him onto the ground.

Suna-kaburi: The spectators closest to the action. It literally means 'to wear sand on your head', as they may be hit by flying sand from the dohyo.

Teppo: To strike yourself with a wooden pole in training to strengthen your arms and shoulders.

Tsuna-tori: The act of tying the white Yokozuna rope around the waist of a newly promoted Yokozuna.

Waza: A technique – such as throwing, tripping or pushing – used to topple your opponent.

Yusho: To win a tournament

TENNIS

PART OF THE UNIVERSAL APPEAL OF TENNIS is that it is really very simple to grasp. You need to hit the ball over the net and into the opposing court within certain lines, without letting the ball bounce twice on your side. The scoring system is a bit fiddlier than it needs to be, and tiebreakers need explaining, while doubles is different (although not by much). Otherwise, it's all pretty straightforward.

Of course, being good at tennis is a whole other ball game. The very best will find the lines with fast first serves and then mix up their second serves with spin and kick. They are equally comfortable on both backhand and forehand.

What's in a name?

One of the problems with tennis language is that it is mighty old, evolving for the best part of a millennium. The derivation of the word 'tennis' itself – whether real, lawn, table or tonsil – is a good example, as nobody really knows where or when it emerged. One thought is that the word travelled north in ancient times from the lost city of Tannis in Egypt. Possible. The most common explanation is the French word *tenez!* – take heed! – was used as a warning to your opponent that you were about to serve. It's just about plausible that French knights in the 1200s, who hit the ball with their hands, would have used this like *en garde!* in fencing. The Italians and English started using variations of *tenez* not long after. The big fly in this ointment, however, is that the French were some of the last in Europe to call it tennis, preferring *jeu de paume* until well into the 19th Century. Curious…

These all-rounders can return with interest, hit heavy groundstrokes from behind the baseline and pick off passing shots, either cross court or down the line. They can drop, smash, volley and lob, all at breakneck speed, on indoor, grass, clay or hard courts, raising their game for the most important points. Damn their eyes! But it does make for great viewing…

Franglais or Double Dutch?

15, 30, 40, game. The scoring system for tennis is second nature to anyone who plays or watches, but it's a bit muddlesome when you think about it. Again, it took root in antiquity (a poem about the Battle of Agincourt in 1415 mentions it) and is also shrouded in mystery. The clock theory is popular, i.e. using the quarter hours on a clock face, with 40 instead of 45 to free up space for *advantage* at 50.

The more likely reason, as with a lot in sport, is gambling. The number 60 was a more important number in olden days France than it is today, and a popular betting coin was the *gros denier tournois*, which was worth 15 deniers. So, a game up to 60 deniers makes sense. The score *forty-five* slimmed down to *forty* over time, simply as an abbreviation. There's every chance too that *advantage* was introduced to up the stakes, both in terms of drama and betting.

Love – for zero – is another teaser. The French word for egg – *L'oeuf* – is tempting, in the same way a duck or '0' in cricket comes from duck egg. The

Talk a good game

Bagel: When the set score is 6–0. A double bagel is 6–0, 6–0 (also called a bicycle), and a triple bagel is just plain unfortunate.

Breadstick: When the set score is 6–1

Paint the lines: To regularly hit the lines. Also *clean the lines*.

Dead Ball: A ball that's patted over the net and begging to be put away.

French never use it though, preferring *zéro*. More likely is a Dutch Flemish word *lof* meaning 'honour'. Again, this is gambling related – if you haven't scored, then you are playing for honour alone. And therefore for 'love not money'. But perhaps it's an old Scots word *luff* meaning *nothing*? Take your pick.

For deuce, you guessed it, there are different schools of thought. Everyone seems to agree that it comes from *deux* meaning two in French. But whether it is short for *a deux de jeu* or *a deux le jeu* splits opinion. The first implies that you are two points from winning the game, the second that you both have an even chance of winning it. Again, the French don't say *deuce*, but they do have two names for it, just to make things more complicated, which you'll hear if you're ever watching the French Open at Roland-Garros. When the players reach deuce for the first time, this is *quarante-a* (short for *quarante-a-quarante* or forty-all). But if the score returns to deuce after an advantage, then it is *égalité* thereafter. Which makes the second interpretation of *deuce* more likely. Perhaps.

Dirtballer: A clay court specialist, traditionally Spanish or French.

Hook: To get caught cheating. Not good.

Ghost into net: To sneak up to the net, when your opponent is concentrating on or chasing down the ball.

Grinder: A *baseliner* who chases everything down, with a view of getting the opponent to play one more ball, frustrating them into a lower percentage forcing shot. The best are *counterpunchers,* suddenly turning defence into attack.

Moonball: Lofted topspin shot, played with gusto, which disrupts the rhythm of your opponent. Supremely annoying and therefore often successful.

Pusher: Derogatory term for someone whose sole aim is to get the ball back in play, without any pace.

Put Away: A ball that is easy to hit for a winner.

Soft hands: To show good touch around the net or in playing delicate drop shots.

Put action on the ball: To spin the ball.

Break back: To break your opponent's serve in the same set, after he has broken yours. Big momentum swing.

Break point: A clutch point, where the receiver has a chance to break his opponent's serve. If the score is 0–40, then you have three break points.

Breaker: Common name for a tiebreak. It's the first to seven, but you have to win by two clear points. The first to serve serves just once, then it is two apiece thereafter. You swap ends after six points.

Brutaliser: To whack the ball directly at your opponent. Won't win you friends, but it will win the point. Also *to tube* your opponent.

Challenge: In leading tournaments, when a player disagrees with the linesman's call and wants a second opinion from HawkEye. If proved wrong, then the point is lost. If correct, and the ball was out, he wins the point. If the ball is called out, but it was then proved to have bounced on the line, then they play the point again. Players get three per set, with an extra challenge in a tiebreaker. Often accompanied by a slow handclap.

Chip and charge: Slicing the ball to the baseline, then sprinting up to the net to force your opponent into a passing shot or lob.

Code violation: Players can have their wrists slapped by the umpire for a number of offences, including delaying play, racquet abuse, shouting obscenities and unsportsmanlike conduct (such as challenging a call when even spectators in

'NEW balls, please.'

row Z knew the ball was out). The first violation is a warning; the second loses a point; on the third, it's a whole game; and with the fourth, you forfeit the match. Physical abuse is an instant default.

Consolidate: To hold serve after a break. An insurance break is to break for a second time, allowing you to lose your own serve once.

Grunt: A yelp of exertion when hitting the ball. Some can be high-pitched and loud, and therefore comical or annoying, depending on their frequency.

Jamming: Serving or returning at the opponent's body, so they can't free their arms.

Junk ball: To deliberately push the ball back without pace or spin to upset your opponent's rhythm. A shallow moonball.

Kick serve: Often a slower second serve, with wicked topspin, that catches the receiver by surprise.

Love game: To win all four points. For big servers, this could be four aces or service winners.

Mini-break: To win a point on your opponent's serve in a tiebreaker. Win two and you might 'take control of the breaker'.

Not up: When the ball has bounced twice. Called by honest players or the umpire.

On serve: When both players are winning their service games. Also 'going with serve'. We're heading to a tiebreaker or long into the night, if it's the deciding set (which must be won by two clear games in Grand Slams).

Overrule: When the umpire, with his or her elevated position, reverses the call made by a linesman.

Poaching: In doubles, when the player at the net moves across sharply to volley a ball headed towards his partner. In recreational tennis, this can cause tension, especially if fluffed into the net.

Sledgehammer: Down the line winner with a two-handed backhand.

Spank: A well-hit groundstroke. 'Boom! She absolutely spanked that.'

Stopper: A player who has the ability to beat a top seed, but is unlikely to go much further. Worth avoiding.

Tank: To stop trying in a couple of games, because you know the set has gone. You can then refresh and serve first in the next set.

Tennis dad: Mischievous term for an overzealous father who pushes his girl prodigy to the limit.

Tweener: To chase down a lob and hit the shot between your legs. Also, a *hot shot*.

Unforced error: To make duff a shot that you ought to have made. Usually a sign of pressure or lost concentration, and critical in the final analysis.

REAL TENNIS

TO LOOK AT, real tennis is like a cross between squash and pinball. For those who play and love the game, there is no finer pursuit in life: an exacting examination of skill, tactics, mental strength and fitness. For those who have never played – there are only 43 courts in the world, so that's most of us – it all looks a bit random.

The game was originally played in monastic cloisters, which had sloping roofs, buttresses, holes, grilles and galleries for the monks to peek through. These features remain, causing the ball to deflect and spin in wicked directions. By hitting certain ones, you can immediately score points, so they need to be defended by your opponent.

The court is asymmetrical: the server serves from the service end, while the receiver receives from the hazard end, which has plenty of them, including a kink in the wall called a *tambour*. The scoring system is largely the same as lawn tennis – indeed, it came first – but it's the first to six games who wins the set, without a tie-breaker. Unlike tennis, the score of the winner is given first, rather than the server.

Again, unlike lawn tennis, your shelf life at the top of the game is far longer. The best players have an endless arsenal of tricks to bamboozle a lesser opponent. Serving alone provides a raft of options, from the *giraffe* (long neck, flying high into the air), the *railroad* (straight, hard and powerful), the *boomerang* (doubles back on itself) and the dastardly *caterpillar*, which bumps along the *penthouses* (sloping roofs along one side). It sounds more like a Sixties play list than top end sport.

What's in a name?

'Disturb'd with chases'

Unlike Real Madrid, the name Real Tennis has nothing to do with its royal roots: it emerged in the 20th century to distinguish it from the newer lawn tennis. Before, it was just called tennis. This ancient version is often referred to as the king of racket sports though, as many monarchs did play, including Henry VIII, who was alleged to have taken to the court to keep his mind busy whilst Anne Boleyn was executed.

Real tennis was certainly known to William Shakespeare, writing several decades later. In his rollicking play *Henry V*, the king is sent a chest of tennis balls as an insult from the Dauphin. Harry has asked for several Dukedoms in France and gets the answer (to paraphrase) 'balls to that!' Angered, the young English king replies to the French ambassador:

His present, and your pains, we thank you for:
When we have match'd our rackets to these balls,
We will, in France, by God's grace play a set,
Shall strike his father's crown into the Hazard:
Tell him, he made a match with such a wrangler,
That all the Courts of France will be disturb'd with chases.

That last word needs some explaining, as it is just about the most complicated word in sport! The *chase* occurs when the ball bounces twice without being returned. The point at which the second bounce falls is recorded, the players then change ends and the opponent attempts to *beat the chase*, by hitting a shot that cannot be returned and whose second bounce is closer to the back wall than that of the chase. Shakespeare was enjoying some poetic licence, as the system of chases is thought to have emerged in Henry VIII's reign, well over a century after Agincourt.

AUSTRALIAN RULES FOOTBALL

AUSSIE RULES – commonly known as *footie* down under – is a national obsession in Australia. It was invented back in the 1850s to combine all of the ball sports of the day, and it remains a combination of soccer and rugby, with elements of basketball, Gaelic football, hockey and volleyball. But for red-blooded, high octane, no-holds-barred mayhem, there's no sport like it. If you haven't watched a game, and you have a spare three hours, then tune in and max out.

The rules are pretty simple. Six-point goals are scored by kicking the ball through the high posts (like rugby posts without a crossbar). You get one point if the ball goes through the smaller outside posts. Teams have 18 players on the field throughout – six forwards, six midfielders and six backmen – with four interchange players who can sub on and off at any time. Players are never booked or sent off in elite contests – although they can have their number taken for future bans – so anything goes. A *bit of biffo* is commonplace, with full-on brawls all part of the family fun.

These basic terms should keep you right.

Talk a good game

Handball: Players can't pass as they would in rugby, but instead they have to punch the ball, like a volleyball player. A handball can go in any direction.

Kicking: Teammates also pass to each other by kicking, and score goals by kicking. Any player can kick and score, so everybody needs to be good at it.

Running: You can run with the ball in hand, in any direction, but you need to bounce the ball every 15 metres – no easy task at full tilt with someone gunning to smash you.

Mark: When a ball is hoofed for more than 15 metres, players from both sides compete to catch it. If someone catches it cleanly, they can't be tackled and have a few seconds' grace to make their next move, if they choose.

Goal: When the ball passes through the two tallest posts in the middle of the goal area the team scores six points. One point is scored should the ball pass between a tall post and the short post on either side.

Sausage roll: Rhyming slang for goal. *Snag* (Aussie for sausage) is also a goal, evolving the same idea.

Tackle: Any player holding the ball is fair game, although tackles must be between the knee and shoulder. Pushing is not allowed.

Inevitably for an Australian sport with a long heritage, the lingo is colourful and descriptive. Here are some fun terms.

Baaaal!: If a player is tackled, he has to let go of the ball. The rival fans shout this to tell the referee they think the player is holding onto it.

Chewy on your boot!: A popular chant to distract a kicker when taking a set shot for goal.

Debacle: A poor performance by your team. You've been 'done like a dinner'.

Dog's eye: Rhyming slang for a meat pie, an integral part of any footy match. *Dead horse?* Tomato sauce.

Falcon: When a player is hit on the *scone* (head) by a stray ball. Probably hurts like hell, but everybody still laughs.

Couldn't get a kick in a street fight: Insult for a player who's struggling to make an impact.

'Chewy on yer boot!'

Jumper punch: An obvious punch will get you banned. Far stealthier to grab the player by his shirtfront and use that hand to punch.

An airy: To *fresh air* the ball when kicking, normally because you've been tackled.

A bagful: To kick a lot of goals.

Shirtfront: To smash into an opponent head-on.

Specky: Short for spectacular. A show-stopping mark. Also a *hanger*.

Aerial ping-pong: When kicks go back and forth.

Selling some candy: To dummy an opponent.

Coathanger: A spiteful tackle using a stiff arm against the ball carrier's neck or head.

Granny: The Grand Final.

Straight down the guts!: What spectators shout if they want you to kick it down the corridor, rather than mess about down the sides.

Hear footsteps: To act rashly like you're about to get clattered, but you have more time than you think.

Maggot: Not-so friendly name for the umpire. *White maggot* is the full title, even though they now wear coloured clothing.

Paddock: The field of play. Also: *oval.*

Prune: The field. Also *pill* or *Sherrin* (popular manufacturer).

Roost: To kick the ball high and long.

Show pony: Any player who looks great when in the clear, but not so clever in the dirty, harder bits.

Stepladder: When a player clambers on another to take a specky.

Yamug: Directed at the umpire, oppo players, your own players, the fella behind you who spills beer on your head.

POLO

POLO MATCHES are extremely social and exciting venues to spend a sunny afternoon. Of course, there are plenty who prefer to chinwag with their backs to the action, but they are missing out on some high octane sport.

The aim is to score more goals than the opposition, hitting the ball through the posts at either end – in that respect, it's sort of Aussie Rules on horseback. The teams swap sides after each goal, and the ball is thrown back in by the umpire. The match is broken into seven-minute *chukkas*, with usually six or eight chukkas in total. Riders will change their ponies after each one. The defending team will try to ride off opponents with their ponies and stop them from hitting the ball forward, which will often need adjudicating for fouls by the umpire.

Playing to your handicap

To even up the sides – and to give wealthy amateurs the chance to play against the top professionals – polo has a handicap system, which has worked pretty well for over a century. Your handicap ranges from minus two to ten. Most novices are rated 0 to –2, while the very best dozen or so players in the world reach the 10-goal level. High-goal players (five and above) tend to be professionals.

It's not the number of goals you are likely to score, but your overall worth to the team in terms of ability, experience and also the ponies at your disposal. When all four team members are added up, you might have a total of five goals. If your opponents totalled eight goals, then you would get a three-goal head start. Having a good low-handicapper in your team can make all the difference.

Talk a good game

Appealing: As with football, players are more likely to a get a decision in their favour if they ask the officials. Claims for a foul are made by lifting the stick (and shouting out what the official should have seen). Excessive appealing can count against you.

Back: There are four players in a team, and the number four is referred to by his position at the back.

Ball: A 3.5-inch diameter plastic or wooden ball that weighs 4.5 ounces. Travels at high speeds, so spectators beware!

Bell or Hooter: Managed by the official timekeeper, it announces when a seven-minute chukka is over.

Boludo: An Argentinian insult, shouted when a teammate or opponent does something stupid or aggravating. Literally, 'big balls', and therefore stupid. Often a rebuke against junior players, but rarely directed against the don paying the bills. English players have adopted it.

Choto: Another choice rebuke. A choto was originally a type of sausage, so you can probably work out its modern meaning. Also used for anything that's a bit rubbish.

Bump: Riding into opposition players to put them off their stroke is integral to any polo match, often done at high speeds with huge force. Of course, there can't be side on collisions – the angle of contact is less than 45 degrees – and sometimes a glancing blow is all that's needed. But polo is certainly a contact sport and players (and their ponies) need to take physical punishment.

Divots: Turf kicked up by ponies' hooves. *Treaded in* by the spectators during the intervals.

Ends: The back line of the field. The teams swap ends after each goal, so that wind and ground doesn't give an unfair advantage.

Field: 300 yards by 160 yards, about the size of three football pitches. The goals are eight yards apart.

Goal: When the ball goes between the sticks, at whatever height. The pony can kick it through too, and often does. This is called a *pony goal*.

High-Goal: When teams total between 17–24 goals.

Low-goal: Teams with a total handicap of 8 goals or less.

Hired Assassin: A trusty pro, usually an Argentinian.

Hook: To obstruct an opponent's shot, with your own stick, as long as you're on the same side of his pony as the ball.

Knock-in: Like a goal kick in football – restarting play from the back of the field when the ball has gone over the end.

Crossing the line: If you are chasing a ball, and closest, then you effectively have right of way. If an opponent crosses the line, obstructing your passage, so to speak, then that's a foul.

Millionaire's shot: A high-tariff shot between the legs of a pony that could end up hurting the poor creature. Only someone with too much money would risk putting an expensive pony on the sidelines.

Near-side: The left-hand side of the pony.

Offside: The right-hand side, which is easier to hit from. Offside in the football or rugby sense doesn't exist.

Patron: The head honcho who funds the team, usually made up of him or herself, two professionals and a pal. They get to name the team whatever they like, because it's theirs.

Penalty: Depending on the severity of the foul, teams are awarded a penalty. This will be an automatic goal for the worst offences, then 30 or 40 yards to an open goal, then a free hit from further out.

Ponies: The real stars of the show. The best will play the game instinctively and seemingly for fun.

Positions: Number 1 is expected to score goals, 2 is the go-between, 3 is the playmaker, while 4 is your defender.

Ringer: A derogatory term for a low handicapper who turns out to be pretty good.

Extra Time: To decide the winner of a tied match, there is a sudden death five-minute chukka, with the goals doubled in width. The first to score wins.

Your line: Shouted to teammates to reassure them they have the line. If it influences the umpire, then so much the better.

Take the man: Shouted when your buddy in front is competing for the ball with an opponent. You want him to ride this player off, because you have the ball in your sights.

ELEPHANT POLO

ELEPHANT POLO is similar to standard polo. The aim of hitting the ball through the goals with a mallet and stopping your opponent is mostly the same. But there is one noticeable difference: they're all riding elephants.

As a consequence, the rules have gradually evolved to make the game fun for the players, exciting for the spectators, but – above all else – safe for the elephants. The World Elephant Polo Association, based in Nepal, donates all proceeds of tournaments to providing Asiatic elephant welfare, sustenance, employment, *mahout* training and medical treatment provision.

There are typically four players per team, who ride elephants allocated from a wide pool to ensure fairness. Actually, they don't ride them – that's the job of the mahout – the player sits behind the mahout so clear communication (or an experienced mahout) counts as much as good stickwork. The field is about a third smaller than in standard polo. Importantly, each team must have at least one elephant in each half at any time to avoid congestion. No more than two elephants may be in the D at one time – one from the attacking team and one from the defending team.

The mallets are two metres long and held on the right-hand side. Women may use two hands if they like, but men just the one, so strong wrists are vital. Teams may not *park the bus* by lying an elephant down in front of the goalmouth. Nelly can't pick the ball up with her trunk either, although she often does – it's a free hit if caught. Handicaps are given to more experienced players – both elephant and equine.

Training isn't easy, so players might limber up by knocking a ball off the side of a jeep. Swinging a golf club in water is another good way to strengthen the wrists. Matches are played with standard polo balls (they tried footballs but the elephants enjoyed popping them), with two 10-minute chukkas. Elephants and ends are changed at half time. There are no restrictions concerning the height, weight or sex of the elephants.

'So much for our star player.'

Talk a good game

Tiger Tops: The Himalayan lodge in Nepal where the World Championship began in 1982.

Sola topee: Pith helmet. Traditionally made from *shola pith* – a dried, milky-white spongy substance made from the shola plant which provides shade from the sun.

Pick-me-up: According to the rules: 'Sugar cane or rice balls packed with vitamins (molasses and rock salt) shall be given to the elephants at the end of each match and a cold beer, or soft drink, to the elephant drivers and not vice versa.'

Standing on the ball: To deliberately position your elephant so the opposition can hit the ball. A foul.

Fouling: Hooking, crossing, dangerous play. Nothing to do with elephant poop.

Ankush: Sharp-tipped billhooks, also known as elephant goads. A cruel way of driving and training elephants. These are banned. Mahouts carry short wooden poles.

SUMMER OLYMPICS

FAIR PLAY, sportsmanship, bringing the game into disrepute – these are all important, but ambiguous terms that have evolved in sport as the stakes have grown. Most sports include a section in their rules and regulations devoted to the 'spirit' or good of the game. They are hard to define, although sportsmen and women tend to know when they've crossed the line.

This intangible ethos of *l'esprit sportif* was foremost in the mind of Baron Pierre de Coubertin, a French ideologue and philanthropist, who revived the Olympic Games at the end of the 19th Century. He passionately believed that everybody in the world had the right to play sport 'without discrimination of any kind and in the Olympic spirit, which requires mutual understanding with a spirit of friendship, solidarity and fair play'. His enthusiasm was often dismissed as boyish and naïve, but eventually he grabbed the attention of enough important people to restage the Games in Athens in 1898, about 2,000 years after their first incarnation in Ancient Greece.

In the decades to follow, de Coubertin's vision has been challenged, often with tragic results. Olympism has been repeatedly corrupted by cheats, and exploited for political gain. Many of the darkest episodes in Olympic history would number among those in all sport.

Yet, for all that de Coubertin might despair at the commercialism of modern Games, his legacy endures and continues to grow. The four-yearly bonanza brings the world together like no other event. For every cynic, there are many thousands who are genuinely invigorated by the Olympic Spirit and its promise of togetherness through sport. If that's naïve, then hey, it's only for a few weeks every four years. Far better to tune in and sport out!

Sports that are widely followed outside the Olympics – golf, tennis, basketball and rugby sevens – already have their own section in the book.

'Anyone got a light?'

Key Olympic terms:

Olympic Truce: The *ekecheiria* (literally 'holding of hands') was a sacred truce that demanded safe passage of athletes to and from the sanctuary of Olympia in Elis. An Olympic Truce Resolution for London 2012 has been signed by all 193 members of the United Nations.

Olympic Creed: 'The most important thing in the Olympic Games is not to win but to take part, just as the most important thing in life is not the triumph but the struggle. The essential thing is not to have conquered but to have fought well.'

Olympic Flag: The interlacing rings represent the five continents, connected in harmony and meeting at the games. The six colours – blue, black, red (on top), yellow, green (below) and the white background – can be found in the flag of each competing nation.

Olympic Oath: 'In the name of all competitors, I promise that we shall take part in these Olympic Games, respecting and abiding by the rules which govern them, in the true spirit of sportsmanship, for the glory of sport and the honour of our teams.'

Olympic Motto: *Citius, Altius, Fortius* (Swifter, Higher, Stronger) was introduced at Paris 1924. For grammar geeks, these are comparative adverbs, not adjectives…

Olympic Flame: In ancient times, a perpetual flame, lit by the rays of the sun, burned at the Olympic sanctuary. The flaming cauldron was reintroduced by Amsterdam in 1928. And in 1936, the Berlin organisers began the traditional torch relay, carrying the flame from Olympia to the host city.

ARCHERY

WHOEVER SCORES THE MOST POINTS WINS THE MATCH. The inner ring of the yellow – the bull's eye – is ten points, with concentric rings scoring one point less the further you miss. If there's a tie in scores, then the archer who has hit a small circle at the centre of the bulls-eye most, called the x10, wins. Archers stand 70 yards away, so it's pretty extraordinary they can hit a 1.2m diameter target, let alone a five pence piece at the centre.

The archers compete in a knock-out, largely based on ranking, with the best reaching the quarter-finals. They then shoot 12 arrows against each other alternatively, in four ends of three, with the drama ratcheting up with every arrow. In team matches, three archers from the same nation shoot eight arrows apiece. The highest combined score wins.

Strong arms and back help, but archery is largely about rhythm and technique under pressure. The best aren't fazed by the situation, able to live in the moment without thinking about the match state or prize.

Talk a good game

Recurve: The bow used at the Olympics, so-named because the extremities of the bow curve away from the archer. This stores much more energy and creates a stronger *twang*. Modern archers love to accessorise, using all manner of gadgets and fiddly bits to balance their bow.

Thumb ring: A leather flap to protect your fingers. The *arm guard* also avoids loss of hair and skin.

Clicker: Repetition is vital for archers. They rely as much on muscle memory and rhythm as aim. Indeed, some fine archers don't have the best eyesight, trusting on feel instead. Archers have a small wire at the front of the bow, which clicks off the arrow when the string is pulled far enough back, so they know when to loose.

Kisser: Also aids repetition. Archers press these little buttons on the string to their lips, so they know they're in position A.

Stabilisers: A bit like kids on their first bike, these rods off to the side help balance and absorb vibrations.

Fast!: A shout that means Stop! No matter who shouts it, everyone lowers their bow and puts arrows back in the quiver.

Burn a hole in the yellow: To focus intensely on the bulls-eye until the string goes twang.

Robin Hood: We've all seen the films – an arrow that pierces the back of another that's already in the centre. A miracle shot.

Grip it and rip it: When you don't clutter your brain with thoughts of technique – you just go shoot.

Jar-licker: To touch the very outside of a line, so you get a higher score. Can be the difference between silver and gold.

Spider: To hit the 'X' that's drawn right at the centre of the bull's eye.

Chunk: The same as golf – to totally lose your form at a critical moment. Risks missing the target altogether.

ATHLETICS

ON THE FACE OF THEM, athletics are the simplest sports known. They connect us to the glory days of the ancient Olympics, when athletes were naked and competed to find the strongest and fastest, and the best jumpers and throwers. Modern athletics, fully clothed and with women too, retains the same adulation of human physical achievement, although the best must also have sound mental toughness and tactical nous.

RUNNING

Sprints: The 100m remains the benchmark for speed. The fastest man or woman in the world is the quickest to cover 100 metres from a static start. The race is often won before the gun, as runners try to out-psych and trash talk an advantage. The 200m is another highlight of the Games. The staggered runners level out after the bend and you start to see who is ahead. The 400m sprint is just brutal. The winner will have courage, as well as raw pace and stamina, as even the best must run through the pain barrier to win.

Relays: Nations then compete over 4x100m and 4x400m relays, which again rely on smooth handovers as much as raw pace, especially in the 4x100m. Do the teams really practise the handovers as much as they could? The regular drops and collisions suggest not...

Hurdles: All races have ten jumps. Men compete over 110m and 400m, while women run 100m and 400m, with rhythm and confidence, and rubber hamstrings.

Middle distance: For 800m and 1,500m (the metric mile), winning now becomes more important than times, although a standout competitor might have a dig at the record. Matching speed with stamina, a street fighter's mentality and sixth sense for when to attack; many of the best mature with age. Runners start in lanes, but break after 100m. The bell sounds before the final lap, often setting the athletes into a mad sprint, as though they'd since forgotten why they were there.

Steeplechase: No longer run between churches, the athletes must still cross 28 stiles (hurdles) and 7 streams (water jumps) over a gruelling 3,000m. The hurdles don't bend, so you'll see most runners land one or two feet on top to avoid smacking their face on the track.

Long distance: It's frankly a wonder how the 5,000m and 10,000m runners keep going so fast for so long. Then still have enough juice in their legs to hammer for home, if needed. Watching these superhumans fight down the home straight of the 5,000m is one of the most rousing scenes at the Olympics. Then some of them do it again in the 10,000m!

Marathon: An event filled with plenty of history and no little scandal. Pheidippides was the unfortunate Athenian soldier who carried news of the victory at Marathon in 490BC, before dying of exhaustion. Some 2,500 years later, athletes are getting ever closer to running the 26 miles and 385 yards in less than two hours.

Walking: Possibly the oddest looking event in track and field, the athletes look like they are late for class, but know they can't run in the corridors. One foot must be on the ground at all times, while the front leg must be straight until it passes the vertical. It's a wonder they keep it up for 20km (men and women) and 50km (just men). In fact, some don't and will be red-flagged for bending the rules (and their legs).

JUMPING

High Jump: The winner is not the person who can jump the highest, but the person who can jump over the highest bar on the day, which is something altogether more taxing. Contenders used to jump forward until Dick Fosbury stunned the world in 1968 by flopping over backwards. Everybody has done the same since.

'If he doesn't get any better, he's for the High Jump.'

Long jump: Successful jumpers display great speed and spring, but also fabulous timing in hitting the 20cm white take-off point at full tilt. If their paw print – even the tiniest toe – appears on the putty, then it's a foul jump. Jumpers get three attempts to qualify for the eight-person final, then another three. The longest jump of the Games – even if it's in qualification – is the winner.

Pole vault: Useful for winning gold medals and escaping prison, the pole vault is another quirky event that captures our attention every four years. The athletes charge towards the bar like they're carrying a very long bayonet, which they stick into a box and then propel themselves upwards as the pole straightens. If they manage to slip over the bar, they often start celebrating on the way down. To conserve energy – and show confidence – they may choose to start at a higher mark than others, although this risks a no-score.

Triple jump: Just to make the long jump more complicated, the athlete must first hop (landing on the same foot), then skip (landing on the other foot) before jumping forward (to land on both feet), whilst not overstepping the board.

THROWING

These ancient disciplines combine strength and speed, creating power and velocity with the body or arm. The winner might simply be the one who wants it the most – there is something elemental and hypnotic about watching these giants leave it all out there. Many start roaring after they have let go as part of their follow through, so that the release is part of the flow, not the stopping point. Throwers get three chances to qualify for the 8-person final, then another three goes. The longest on the day wins.

Discus: If you had to choose one event to represent Olympism, then it might well be the discus. Unlike the javelin, shot or hammer, the discus appears to have evolved for sporting reasons in ancient times, rather than military. From 1900, athletes began spinning around to create more velocity. Men throw 2kg discs, while women's are 1kg. For trivia buffs, this is the only track and field event in which the women's world record is superior to the men's.

Javelin: Throwing a spear was a practical skill for ancient Greeks. Of course, in battle, the ability to make it drop with the point down could be the difference between life and death, rather than gold and silver. In modern athletics stadia, the field events take place inside the track, so it's important the javelin is thrown safely A strong fast arm is key, but also coordination, timing and controlled aggression.

Shot put: Most cultures have a history of competitive stone throwing, although 'putting' heavy weights as a strength contest was especially popular in the Scottish Highlands. The *shot* refers to cannon balls, and today's metal missiles weight 7.26kg and 4kg for men and women respectively. The athletes must throw straight-armed from the chin and create momentum by backing across the circle or spinning, and then jamming their foot against a stop board. Get sconed by one of these and the lights go out.

Hammer: Another favourite of Highland Games, the hammer is effectively a shot put on the end of a wire. The thrower spins round four times, before letting go with a roar. This projectile can end up over 80 metres away or lodged in the roof of the protective net with everybody ducking for cover.

COMBINED EVENTS

Decathlon/Heptathlon: The event to find the best all-round athlete, capable of sprinting, middle distance, hurdling, throwing and jumping. Men do ten events: 100m, long jump, shot put, high jump and 400m on the first day; then 110m hurdles, discus, pole vault, javelin and 1500m on the second. Women's heptathlon (seven events) is 100m hurdles, shot put, high jump and 200m; then long jump, javelin and 800m. No wonder some of the competitors fall over the line at the end. Whoever accumulates the most number of points wins. Pacing yourself, depending on the competition, is key to winning – that, and being superhuman.

BADMINTON

BADMINTON really ought to be more popular than tennis. It needs less space, the equipment is cheaper, it's easier to play too, just as exciting, faster and so better for fitness, and you can belt the shuttlecock without stopping the match to find it. Of course, in the Far East, it *is* much more popular than tennis, which is why they clean up at the Olympics.

As well as power and stamina, badminton is also a game of tactics, touch and deception. The best players rarely out-blast or out-pace each other, so they need to ease their opponent out of position with deft of hand. Veiled drop shots, last-moment flicks, devilish spin can all engineer a small opening for a winning dink or force the other into a lob, which will be smashed at speeds of over 155 mph, with both feet off the ground.

Doubles badminton accentuates the need for clever manoeuvring. Teams will try to victimise a weaker player, as you might expect. The Olympics aren't meant to be polite. If this means peppering the lady in a mixed doubles match, then so be it. But playing the player, not the situation will often backfire…

Talk a good game

Balk: To trick the receiver with a cunningly disguised serve, so they fluff their return.

Birdie: Another name for the shuttlecock.

Block: Like a drop volley in tennis, the birdie is dinked back over the net with a flick of the wrists.

Carry: If you catch the shuttle on your strings then sling it back, that's not OK.

What's in a name?

East to West and back again

Games with shuttlecocks were played in the East for 2,000 years before the Europeans caught the craze in the 16th Century. In Britain, we called it Battledore (stout wooden frames with a hide covering used for beating linen) and Shuttlecock (a missile that shuttled back and forward with cock feathers to help it fly). It wasn't very competitive though – children especially would try to see how long they could keep it moving, whilst singing rhymes.

In the second half of the 19th Century, British officers in India started playing a local game called *poonai* played with floaty woollen balls, nets and line markings. Now, battledore was a favourite of the Duke of Beaufort' children, who lived at Badminton House in Gloucestershire. Their record for rallies in 1830 was 2,117, which takes some counting, let alone doing. The story goes that during a rainy garden party in the 1860s, some officers took refuge indoors and started playing *poonai* by using the children's shuttlecock. It caught on, and when readers of *The Field* magazine began debating the correct rules of the 'Badminton game of battledore' in 1873, the name stuck. A certain Major Forbes sent *A Handbook of Badminton* to the magazine's readers later that year, which made it all official. This formula was then circulated round the globe, regaining its ancient birthright in the Far East.

Drive: A hard-hit shot. One of the most common plays.

Drop: As the name suggests, you want the shuttlecock to land just the other side of the net, forcing your opponent to lob, so you can smash.

Flick: To whip the bird hard with your lower arm at the last moment, just as your opponent thinks you're going for a drop shot.

Funky doubles: When any players can form a doubles pair. Not something you see in the Olympics.

Game: Out of courtesy, you should tell your opponent when you're serving for the game, or indeed the match. A bit like the gesture for 'new balls' or a 'let' in tennis. The players are being polite, but it's not heart-felt.

Jump smash: A shot you see a lot – when the smasher has leapt in the air to generate power.

Kill: A decisive shot that ends the rally.

Rotation: The rhythmic back and forward of a well-drilled pair, who must take alternate shots.

Tumble drop shot: To hit a drop shot in a way that the shuttlecock flips over, rather than the usual cork-first trajectory.

Volleyball/ Beach Volleyball

BEACH VOLLEYBALL is often celebrated for its court-side razzmatazz and ogling opportunities, but it has been a competitive and hard-fought sport since the start of the 20th Century, originating in Hawaii. The basic premise of beach volleyball is to make the ball hit the sand inside your opponent's court, whilst stopping it from hitting yours. Each pair has a maximum of three touches, before the ball is returned to the other side. They then get three touches to send it back with interest.

In an ideal play, the three contacts will be a *dig* (flipping the ball with your forearms to your partner, so stopping the opposition's smash or serve from hitting the sand), then a *set* (nudged upwards by your partner so that the ball hangs by the net), followed by the *attack* (it's your go again, and you slap the ball one-handed over the net). Movement and fitness in the sand is therefore critical, as the players are up and down, diving and leaping, several times in a rally.

Players can also block by jumping up with their hands high. If the ball plops back onto your opponent's side, then that's a point. If it ricochets to your partner, then you still get three more touches on your side.

What else? Players must hit the ball at all times – they can't palm or scoop it. You can't touch the net yourself, but if the ball does then it's still in play. Games are the first to 21 points, by two clear points. Best of three games, with the third acting as a tiebreaker, where the first team to 15 points wins. Teams swap sides on multiples of seven, and on multiples of five in the tiebreaker. Whichever team wins the rally scores a point and serves next.

In the more traditional volleyball, which has been in the Games for longer (but doesn't now get the same airtime for some reason…), teams have six on each side, although it's still just three contacts apiece. Blocking is a key aspect of the game, while players tend to man different zones, which means communication is vital.

Again, the team that wins the point serves next. If they served previously it will be the same player to serve, if not it is rotated to the next player. Matches are the best of five sets. Twelve competing nations are split into two groups of six before quarter-finals, semi-finals and a final. Brazil, Russia and the US are always up there or there about.

Talk a good game

Bambi: Derogatory term for a mild-mannered player.

Dink: To look like you're going to hit the ball hard, but then flick the ball softly over the blockers and drop it onto the sand behind them.

Facial: To get whacked in the face by the ball. Also called a *six-pack*. If it leaves a mark, it's called a *tattoo*. A *chester* hits you in the chest, obviously.

Heater: A well-hit spike.

Wipe: To intentionally hit the ball into a blocker, so it ricochets out and you win the point.

Jed: Another name for a block.

Kong: A one-handed block.

Lip: A dig shot that gets respect from the crowd.

Missile: To hammer a spike or serve over the back. Sounds impressive, but isn't.

Pancake: To dive forward and dig the ball with the back of your hand.

Roof: A block that goes straight down and into the opponent's court, winning the point.

Tool: Not so good. Your block sails out of bounds.

Campfire: When the ball lands between two players, who are both left staring at the mark where it lands.

Spade: Service ace.

Butter: A set that puts the ball on a plate. Also called *nectar*.

Husband and Wife: When the ball drops between two players and they don't communicate properly, so the point is lost. Ouch!

Juice Head: A knucklehead body builder on the beach.

Picnic ball: A game played by people who don't know the rules, so anything goes.

Popcorn: When your partner is setting the ball in all directions (like popcorn in a pan). Also called *sprinkling*.

Rock: Euphemism for a male player who should probably wear a T-shirt. A woman would be a *stone*.

Spike: To smash the ball with one hand. If it slams into the sand to score a winner, then that's a *kill*.

Sky ball: A high, lobbing serve. A variation of the devilish *moonball* in tennis.

Volley Dolley: A girl who likes to hang around volleyball courts.

Whale: To spike the ball as hard as possible, just for the hell of it. A *Prince of Whales* does it all the time.

BOXING

SPECTATORS TEND TO FIND BOXING FASCINATING or gruesome to watch, albeit that Olympic bouts are less vicious than their professional equivalents. There are fewer rounds – three three-minute rounds for men and four two-minute rounds for women – with more of an emphasis on scoring points than hurting the opponent. Without the huge prize money, television freak shows and trash talking, Olympic boxing is more about technique than bravado.

All the same, they are still trying to knock each other's lights out. When you think that most other sports are doing what they can to avoid head injuries, it's not hard to see why boxing has its detractors. Yet, it's also not hard to appreciate the skill, fitness and courage of top fighters. Men compete in 10 weight classes, from light flyweight (49kg) through middleweight (75kg) and up to super heavyweight (above 91kg), while female boxers contest three weight divisions, flyweight (51kg), lightweight (60kg) and middleweight (75kg). Boxers score one point for every punch they land with the marked part of their glove on their opponent's head or upper body. Three of the five judges need to agree for a point to be awarded.

The boxer who wins the round receives ten points, while the loser gets nine (which explains why the scores are so close, even in a one-sided fight). From Rio 2016 onwards, men no longer wear head-guards, which is believed to aid safety, as the boxers have better vision and learn to defend better. On the flip side, the risk of eye cuts may lead to the best boxers retiring early.

Talk a good game

Throw in the towel: When the *cornerman* (usually the trainer) literally throws in a white towel to signal that his man or woman has had enough.

'I can't do the rematch on Wednesday. I've got poetry.'

Seconds out: The command for a boxer's team – his seconds – to leave the ring before the round.

Go the distance: To fight all the rounds without a knock-out.

Southpaw: A left-hander.

Belt: An imaginary line around the boxer's mid-rift – below the belt is illegal. Also *a low blow.*

Jab: Originally a Scottish word meaning to thrust or pierce, the punch is made with a straight-arm, and good for keeping your opponent at arm's length. Good jabbers create a lot of power.

Uppercut: To swing up at your opponent's chin.

Hook: A sideways blow, with the elbow bent, aimed at the opponent's chin or ear.

Standing count: When the referee counts – usually to eight or ten – to give a boxer a chance to recover. If the referee thinks he looks too groggy, then he can stop the contest. To beat the count is to be back on your feet and ready before the ref finishes. Out for the count is a boxer that doesn't.

On the ropes: To be literally pushed back against the ropes of the ring and facing defeat.

Handshake: Touching knuckles before the first round.

Chin: Not just the part of the body, but the ability to take a punch. 'Leading with the chin' is to leave yourself open – ballsy, but potentially foolhardy. To have *no chin* or *a glass chin* is someone who cuts a dash, but gets knocked out easily. Derivation of *take it on the chin* and *chin up!*, although neither of them are ever much consolation.

Pull one's punches: To use less force or show leniency. Not always a bad technique in the Olympics, as accuracy is often more important than hurting the opponent.

Milling: An old army term for boxing, once a compulsory sport.

Dancing: The fancy footwork of the pugilist.

Sunday punch: To knock the opponent into next Sunday. A boxer who knows he is behind on points may be forced to go for a Sunday punch to have any chance of winning.

Peek-a-boo: To have your hands in front of your face as a guard.

Pitty-pat: To score points, but not threaten the safety of your opponent.

Tomato can: A boxer who routinely gets beaten up and dented.

Saved by the bell: When the end of a round arrives just before the knock-out blow.

Sucker punch: An unexpected blow, often against the run of play.

Wind: The boxer's puff or stamina.

CANOEING

THERE ARE TWO DISTINCT TYPES OF CANOEING in the Olympics – slalom and sprint. The slalom, like its alpine cousin, takes the competitor down a course of gates, with the winner successfully negotiating the course in the quickest time. Sprinting is across flat water – a bit like rowing, but in a canoe. Again, the fastest wins the race.

Both events are split into two disciplines: kayaking and, somewhat confusingly, canoeing. In reality, the difference is easy to spot. In kayaking, the athletes have a horizontal two-spaded paddle, while in canoeing, it's a shorter paddle held vertically with one blade. Think *Last of the Mohicans*. Oddly, women are only allowed in the kayak races (and it's a big bone of contention).

In the slalom, competitors will get time penalties for missing a gate, or going through in the wrong direction. Sprints can be solo, pairs races or in teams of four, set over 200m, 500m and 1,000m. Although known as flatwater, the course is at the mercy of weather conditions, with some athletes better in choppier water. Sprinters usually have upper bodies like Tarzan.

Talk a good game

Two: A two-second penalty for touching a pole

Eddy: A white water feature downstream from an obstacle.

Drop: A fall of water creating fast current and tough eddies.

Gates: There are 25 sets of hanging poles, painted red or green according to whether they have to be negotiated downstream (green) or upstream, against the current (red). There are a minimum of six upstream gates, which are harder to tackle. The last gate is always 25m from the finish.

Paddler: The canoeist.

Catch and pull: The technique of canoeists in sprints, using the blade to propel themselves through the water.

Wing paddle: A spoon-shaped paddle, which has recently revolutionised the sport.

Cockpit: Where the paddler sits. Canoeists kneel in canoe sprints.

Cycling

CYCLING IS NOW ONE OF THE BIG EVENTS at the Olympics, set across different disciplines: BMX, downhill, road and track. Here's a whistle-stop tour of what to expect.

BMX

Originating as a way for kids to mimic their motocross heroes on their push bikes – hence the full name bicycle motocross (BMX) – the sport is now a global phenomenon, across both freestyle (street jumps etc) and racing. The Olympics feature the racing version, set over a short, tight, twisting circuit with multiple turns and jumps. Eight riders compete in each race. The first two go through to the next round until they reach the medal race. Big crashes and big air!

Doubles or whoops: Very steep jumps, in pairs. Quick riders will expect to jump both at the same time.

Holeshot: To lead after a fast start. Strong riders will lead to the end.

Wheelie: To have your front wheel in the air, whilst still pedalling.

Manual: To do a wheelie, but without pedalling, i.e. freewheeling.

MOUNTAIN BIKING

This is a physically brutal event. Riders must tackle a number of laps of a course (50km for men, 40km for women) set up by a sadist, across steep climbs, sharp drops, jumps, fallen trees, loose stones and water obstacles. Whoever finishes first gets gold and will have earned it.

A good bike is vital, so riders need to decide between a lightweight steed that's faster, but might need running repairs, or a heavier bike that's more robust and comfortable. The start of the race usually has the best crashes.

Riding hardtail: Without suspension on the back wheel to save on weight.

Bunny-hop: To jump the bike, without dismounting, over an obstacle.

Push-climb: Where the cyclists need to dismount and carry their bikes, usually because it's too rough or steep.

Snakebite: To puncture the tyre by jamming the rim against the rubber in hitting an obstacle. Cyclists must change the tube themselves.

ROAD RACE

This is like a single stage of the Tour de France – indeed with many of the same riders – set across 250km for men and 140km for women. With a number of different riders in each nation's team, it's usually the top sprinter who wins, although a breakaway can clinch it, if enough opposition riders are prepared to go together. Riders must decide how long to stay in the *peloton* before attacking.

TIME TRIAL

Pretty straightforward – all the riders take on the same track – 44km for men and 29km for women – and the fastest wins. There is no racing, per se, as the riders start 90 seconds apart. Riders wear the comedy conical hats to counter wind resistance.

TRACK

Track sprint: A 'best of three' race in the Olympics between two riders over a fixed distance. It starts as a game of cat and mouse, before the final decisive sprint, in which the pursuer tries to draft the leader and overtake before they cross the line.

Track stand: When the sprinters come to a complete standstill, balancing their bikes on the bank. City commuters will do the same at traffic lights.

Pursuit: Individuals or teams start at opposite sides of the track. It looks like they're chasing each other, but they're really racing the clock. The winner advances to the next round.

Keirin: A quirky race in the Olympics where the riders follow a small motorbike (known as a Derny) for several laps, steadily increasing in speed. With two and half laps left, the pacer makes way, and they all sprint to the finish. Meaning 'flying

RAISE YOUR GAME

wheels', the keirin was invented in Japan and remains a hugely popular gambling sport there, similar to horse racing.

Omnium: From Latin for 'of all', it's a points race in the Olympics to find the best all-round rider, with different tests, from sprints to longer distance endurance trials. The points are awarded in reverse order for each race within the race, so the overall winner has the lowest points total.

Elimination: Also known as *Devil Take the Hindmost* or just *The Devil*, the backmarker at the end of each lap is eliminated. The final handful of riders race to the finishing line.

Team sprint: Also known as the *Olympic sprint*, teams of three race against the clock. One rider peels off after each lap, leaving the anchorman to hammer home.

What's in a name?

Madison: This is no longer an Olympic discipline, but it's still a very interesting story. A frenetic long-distance pairs race, in which the teams take it in turns to compete for points, the Madison is best known for the sight of partners 'hand-slinging' each other forward when they swap over. The name itself has a macabre past. It hails from Madison Square Garden in New York, which was a popular velodrome at the end of the 19th Century. Ruthless *six-day races* were a highlight of the sporting and gambling calendar. Riders would try to complete as many laps as possible in 24 hours. The prize money and punters' stakes were so high that riders were expected to push themselves to the brink, often juiced up to the eyeballs. Spectators used to revel in watching these ghost-like figures, 'hideous with the tortures that rack them', according to the *New York Times* in 1897. When a law was decreed to protect the riders, the organisers simply made it a pairs event so that the distances covered were even greater. And so the sling-shotting began. The Madison is known as the *American Race* on the Continent.

DIVING

AS A KID, who hasn't charged up the steps to the 10m platform at a pool with the intention of swan diving majestically into the water below; but then chickened out by falling like a stone feet first, or climbing back down again? The point is that it isn't too hard to empathise with – and deeply respect – the skills and audacity of top class divers. Even the thought of somersaulting off the 3m springboard will set the non-diver's tummy spinning.

At the Olympics, clearly, they have no such qualms. Athletes compete individually and in *synchro* (pairs), with points awarded for technique and aesthetics, with more difficult skills getting proportionally more points. Dives include front, back, reverse, inward, twist and the scary looking armstand, where they have to perch on the edge with their feet towards the ceiling, as if it wasn't difficult enough already. And like when playing duck dives with stones in a river, the less splash the better.

Scoring is quite complicated, but purposely so to avoid national bias and reward ambitious dives. Only five of the seven judges' scores count (the highest and lowest are discarded), then the final figure is multiplied by the *difficulty tariff*, ranging between 1–5.

Talk a good game

Pike: The body is bent at the hips with the legs straight and the toes pointed

Elevation: The height a diver achieves from a take-off.

Approach: The walk or run to the edge before take-off.

Entry: The best entries are made vertically, with no splash.

Bingo: When all the judges award the same score for a particular dive in a contest.

Crimping: To slightly bend your knees in a pike. If the knees are obviously bent, then you're in a *puck*.

Gainers: Reverse dives.

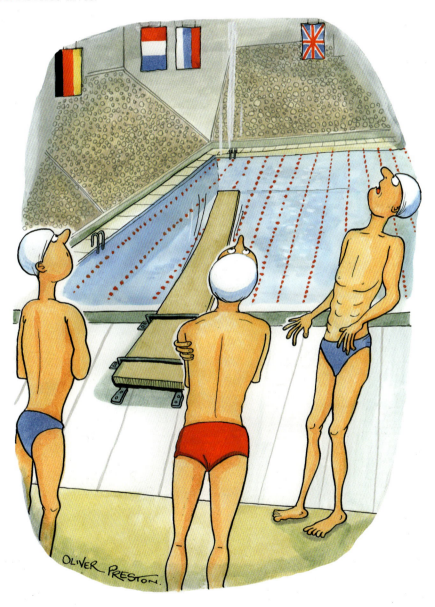

'He said he'd hit the roof if he didn't get this one right.'

Rip entry: To slide into the water without a splash. A really smooth entry is called a *smoke*.

Smack: A belly or back flop. Nasty.

Tower: Diver's name for the platform.

Twister: One of the most difficult dives, therefore the potential to score high or bomb out. Two and a half back-somersaults with two and a half twists.

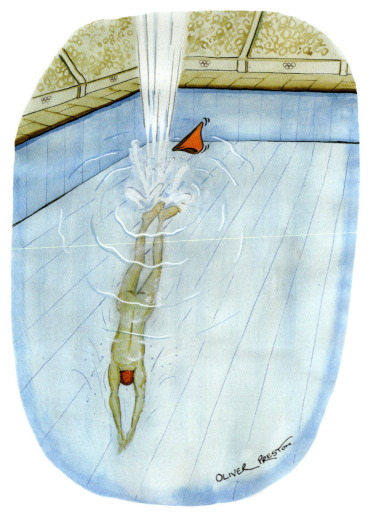

'*Rip entry*'

EQUESTRIANISM

QUESTION: Which is the only Olympic sport in which men and women compete on equal terms? Answer: Equestrianism.

It's not the only event with horses though – they crop up in the Pentathlon too. But such is the importance of the animal on the given day in the specific environment; it's not unusual that many of world's finest riders never taste success at the Olympics, while home advantage can prove critical.

There are three disciplines: dressage, showjumping and then eventing, which combines the first two with a cross-country time trial.

143

DRESSAGE

Moving between letters around a 60 x 20-metre sand-based arena, the horses and riders are tested across a series of movements. The first two rounds are the same for all the riders. The final round, set to music, is a freestyle showcase, where the rider chooses the moves they do best. Judges mark the card according to accuracy of movement, calmness, suppleness and flexibility.

SHOWJUMPING

Once a mainstay of prime time TV, showjumping captures the nation's imagination every four years, and we all wonder why we don't watch it more often. It's really exciting. The riders put their horses across 15 or so jumps, attempting to avoid penalty points for knocking down a pole or going too slow. The winner has the least poles down in the quickest time, so going last can be an advantage.

EVENTING

A cumulative scoring event, with the lowest number of penalty points for the gold medallist. Horse and rider must show finesse in a dressage test, courage and stamina on the cross-country course, and then accuracy under pressure in the showjumping.

Talk a good game:

Aid: A prompt, either using the hands, legs, voice or shifting the seat, to tell the horse to turn or change gait.

Gait: The speed and step sequence of the horse: walk, extended walk, trot, extended trot, canter, gallop.

Half-pass: Balletic movement, both forwards and sideways.

Piaffe: Trotting, but almost on the spot. The legs are going, but they've hardly moved forward.

Run-out: When the horse decides at the last moment not to jump, but to run around the side of an obstacle. If the rider has committed, it can get ugly.

Refusal: The horse may also opt to stop at the base of the jump, causing the jockey to ride up by its ears.

Obstacle: A fence or jump, such as a ditch, rail, table or coffin (rails-ditch-rails).

Walk the course: Eventers will walk round the course on foot, so they know the best angles and the lay of the land.

Obstacles always have a white flag to the left and a red flag to right, so you know which direction to jump.

Optimum time: The notional time which acts as par for time on the course. Too slow and the rider receives penalty points.

Jump judges: The unsung heroes who monitor the jumps through wind, rain and occasional shine.

Clear round: A round without any faults.

Jump-off: When the leaders end on the same number of points. The course is often made shorter and higher to find a winner, against the clock.

Passage: This is a very collected, cadenced trot that is characterised by elevated movement of the knees and hocks, as well as a defined engagement of the quarters.

Change of Lead: The horse is brought from a canter to a few strides of trot and then asked to canter again on the opposite leading leg. A *flying change* is a change of leg whilst cantering. Fancy footwork!

Serpentine: When the horse performs half circles followed by straight lines.

Volte: A 6, 8 or 10m circle. It becomes a circle if the diameter is greater than 10m.

Bounce: A jump that is close together so that the horse can't take a full stride.

FENCING

A GRACEFUL SPORT THAT BELIES ITS SAVAGE HISTORY, where thrusts and lunges were designed to cut, maim and kill the opponent, rather than set off a buzzer. Today's duels still make for a fascinating spectacle, as the fencers move with dazzling footwork and blurring blades to protect themselves, and then score hits on the opponent.

Competitors have a 14m long combat zone, and their swords and sometimes their *lamé* (suit) is *tethered* into the electronic scoring system to show if they have hit or been hit. It's the first to 15 points or the leader after three rounds of three minutes.

Probably the most important bit to understand is the difference between *épée*, sabre and foil.

Foil: This is the nobleman's old training sword – short, lightweight and flexible. Points are scored with the tip of the blade on your opponent's plugged-in *lamé*, which covers the torso from shoulders to groin in the front, and to the waist in the back. The arms, head, neck, and legs are considered off target. There's a coloured light for hits, and a white light for misses.

Épée: A heavier duelling sword, built to keep surgeons and undertakers in business: stiffer, thicker and generally nastier than the foil. Again, only the tip of the blade counts, but fencers can strike anywhere on the body to score, as well you might if fighting to the death. The sword has a blunt tip, which recedes when struck against the body of the opponent, so there's no need for electrified *lamés*, but for plenty of force.

Sabre: Think slashing cavalryman's sword. The fencer can use both tip and blade to score points. And like the hussar on horseback, the target area is above the waist, on the *lamé*, excluding the hands but including the head, which is also wired up.

Talk a good game

Foible: The flexible half of the blade further away from the hilt. The *forte* is the stiffer half closest to the hilt.

Lunge: A well-balanced move forward, allowing the chance to recoil in an instant.

Parry: To deflect an attack, using your forte against their foible.

Riposte: An offensive move, after a parry.

Counter-riposte: To parry the riposte, and riposte yourself.

Flêche: To attack your opponent, often in mid-air, whilst passing them on the piste.

En garde: The preparatory stance.

Feint: To attack down one line, but then switch to another at the last moment.

Mal-parry: When your parry attempt doesn't work.

Brutality: When the fencer dishes out unnecessary pain. It's like they're enjoying it.

Froissement: Often seen in Musketeer movies, the act of disengaging swords from 'forte to foible' when they are locked together. D'Artagnan will send his opponent's sword rattling across the courtyard in a froissement. Then likely give it back.

FIELD HOCKEY

THE TERM 'FOOTBALLERS WITH WEAPONS' is helpful in a sense that it describes the general idea of passing, tackling and shooting to get the ball into a net at one end. Of course, the one part of your body you really mustn't use is your foot.

The sport has transformed in the last two decades to become gut-bustingly fast-paced to play and exciting to watch. The action rarely stops, with players allowed to take *hits* (restarts) to themselves or wherever the ball is, rather than the old days when they returned to the mark and the opposition encircled them on a muddy, bobbly turnip field. There are no offsides either, so defence can switch to attack in the blink of an eye.

The water-based synthetic pitches reward fast, skilful stick work, perpetual substitutions keep the players fresh. Green, yellow and red cards, plus the threat of short corners and penalty flicks, have turned the hackers into dinosaurs.

Talk a good game

D: Some things haven't changed. A goal can only be scored from inside this semicircle, and by an attacking player.

Penalty corner: Like a special play in American sports, a *short corner* is awarded for a foul in the D, and outside it if it's serious enough. Five defenders line up on the backline – some now wear masks to protect their faces – until the ball is pushed to a receiver at the edge of the D. They then charge out or mark other players, while the recipient either takes a shot or sets up a planned move. The goalie, in full battle armour, will rush the shot taker or loiter round the goal. One criticism is that the penalty corner is now so effective that players will try win a short rather than try scoring from open play.

Penalty strokes: For serious offences, especially when defending a shot on goal. They're taken from 6.4m in front of the goal. The taker can only take one step before flicking or pushing the ball, and the keeper can't move until the ball is touched.

Green card: A minor offence that doesn't quite merit a yellow. But two greens is a yellow.

Yellow card: Into the sin bin, you go. The player gets at least five minutes – it could be longer if the umpire isn't feeling generous, or the same player has repeat offended, but doesn't deserve a red card.

Red card: For a particularly nasty challenge or abusing a ref. Permanent exclusion.

Upper V: The best players will target the top corners of the goal.

Drag flick: A powerful stroke, used often in penalty corners, in which the player stands with legs wide apart and creates huge speeds by transferring weight through the body and into the stick, lifting the ball over or past the onrushing keeper.

GYMNASTICS

ONE OF THE PUREST FORMS OF ATHLETICISM shown at the Olympics, the best gymnasts must possess coordination, speed, strength, courage, stamina and the ability to smile when they don't get the score they expected. Men flex their muscles on the floor, pommel horse, rings, vault, parallel bars and horizontal bar, while women contort and fly on the vault, uneven bars, balance beam and floor.

The teams go out first, which also acts as qualification for the individual apparatus final (eight athletes) and the individual overall title (24 athletes). A gymnast could therefore do a large number of performances and win a clutch of medals, and indeed many often do.

APPARATUS

Rings: Two parallel rings 50cm apart, suspended from a cable and straps and held, one in each hand, for a series of exercises, particularly requiring stillness of the body.

Uneven bars: The top bar is 2.4m above the floor, and the lower bar is 1.6m high. Women gymnasts are scored for a continuous series of grip changes, releases, new grasps and other complex moves.

High bar: As the name suggests, this horizontal bar stands 2.75 metres high, and the men swing round, leap, twist and catch it again like chimps on holiday.

Parallel bars: Two wooden rails on uprights, adjustable in height and used for swinging, vaulting and balancing exercises in men's artistic gymnastics. The bars don't bend, so the athletes need to.

Pommel: A solid apparatus on stilts that's 115cm high with two handles, or pommels. The men do a series of manoeuvres defined by complex hand placements and body positions while holding themselves above the apparatus. Extraordinary strength and control are required. Most of us would struggle to climb on top of it.

Vault: A solid apparatus similar to the pommel horse, but lacking handles, and used in both men's and women's gymnastics for a variety of handsprings from a running approach.

Balance beam: A solid platform that's 5 metres long, just 10cm wide, and raised 125cm off the ground. Somehow, the women cartwheel, hop and flip on top, before a theatrical dismount.

Floor: The floor exercise is one of the highlights for both men and women. The springy surface allows them to tumble and somersault with gusto. The women do their routines to music, the men in silence.

Talk a good game

Gymnastics: The word derives from the Greek word *gymnos* meaning naked, because that's how they competed, back in the day.

Rhythmic gymnastics: This is just for the women, and comprises two competitions – individual and team. Always with music, the gymnasts show their skills with a rope, hoop, ball, clubs or satin ribbon, and are marked out of 30 on technical ability, artistic interpretation and execution.

Salto: A flip or somersault where the gymnast rotates around the axis of their hips.

Arabesque: A position where the gymnast balances on one leg with the other leg raised and extended behind the body in a split.

Perfect dismount: Getting off the apparatus to end the routine, in an impressive and stable way.

Trampoline: A discipline of its own, with medals for the highest scoring individuals. It's sort of a cross between gymnastics and diving, reaching extraordinary heights. Of course, aside from the athleticism, part of the skill is hitting the canvas at the right angle and speed to get high enough for the next wave of dazzling skills. The different moves tend to have men's names, after the people who made them famous, like the *Barani* – a forward somersault with a half-twist, named after the 19th Century Italian circus star Alfonso Barani. You'll also see a *Cody, Randy, Rudy* and *Adolph*. A *ball-out* is a one and a quarter front somersault taking off from a back-drop position, not a wardrobe malfunction.

Tumbling: Acrobatic skills, such as back handsprings and saltos. A tumbling run is one of the highlights of the floor exercise.

HANDBALL

LOVERS OF HANDBALL – and there are plenty worldwide – will tell you their cherished sport is a mix between football, basketball, water polo and indoor hockey, but faster, more demanding and more exciting than all of them combined. It's certainly a high scoring fest, as players pass the ball (bit smaller than a football) by hand to one-another, with a view to getting within range of the goal (similar to a hockey goal) and then winging the ball like a thunderbolt into the net. They can run with the ball – bouncing it every three strides – although they can expect to get clattered if they hold onto it for too long: handball is most definitely a contact sport. So we can maybe throw in Aussie Rules as another sport that handballers would perceive as similar but inferior.

Here are the basics. Teams of seven, with a full-time goalie, play indoors with nets at both ends. Blocking is allowed at any time on any player, as long as you don't use your arms, legs, feet or hands, so there are some high impact body slams and collisions. Players are not allowed to enter the goalie's semi-circle, although there is a big BUT to this rule. They are not deemed to have entered until their feet touch the ground, so a typical scoring play is to enter the circle in mid-air, on your third step, then launch the ball just before you land.

Watching the goalie doing his best to block the ball – often with his face – is one of the most forlorn sights in sport. Penalty shots from 7m away are especially one-sided in favour of the attacker. But with margins tight, the plucky, unhinged goalie can end up the hero.

Talk a good game

Pivot: A bit of a goal-hanger, this assassin needs to be on the money more times than not.

Passive play: As if handball wasn't fast enough, a team can lose possession for appearing to have a bit of a breather or running down the clock. The ref will warn them, then hand the ball over.

Jump Shot: An attempt to score, usually leaping into the semi-circle.

Drawer: The top corner of the net.

Vaseline: When the goalie makes himself as big as possible, trying to reach all four corners with his four limbs.

JUDO

MEANING THE 'GENTLE WAY' IN JAPANESE, judo is the thinking man's jujitsu, although you need plenty of strength and agility to back up the mind games. The idea is to read your opponent, then use their weaknesses against them to take them down or immobilise them. That said, the best will empty their minds and react to their opponent's movements instinctively. So, in a way, they learn to think so clearly, they don't need to think any more.

Bouts can last up to five minutes, with points and penalties awarded along the way, although the competing *judokas* aim to force a win earlier. There are plenty of Japanese terms, but you can get by with just a few.

Talk a good game

Ippon: A controlled throw that lands an opponent on their shoulder. This wins the bout immediately. Pinning an opponent on their back or forcing them to submit to a choke, arm-lock or strangle will also be rewarded with a decisive ippon.

Waza-ari: A common way to score points, throwing your opponent on their back, but without the force or control to get an outright ippon.

Yuko: To throw your opponent on their side. Only really matters if the scores are tied, and the fighters are in a *Golden Score* tiebreaker.

Rei: Bow – the judokas do this at the beginning and end.

Hajime: The command to start, by the *shinpan* (referee).

Soremade: the command to stop.

Judogi: Or just *Gi*. The jacket, which often comes undone at the belt, allowing extra purchase to grapple.

Sensei: The teacher

Tatami: The mat

MODERN PENTATHLON

THE MODERN PENTATHLON – five events: fencing, swimming, riding, running and shooting – is a very Olympic thing. It was one of the many brainchildren of the founder of the Games, Baron Pierre de Coubertin, who was ever so slightly obsessed by Ancient Greece. The original version of the Pentathlon – long jump, javelin, discus, running in armour and wrestling in one day – was designed to test the warrior skills of athletes. Such was its prominence that the winner was proclaimed the *Victor Ludorum* (winner of the games), or the Greek equivalent. The goodly Baron adapted the event for a 19th Century messenger or spy, riding behind enemy lines, who might be expected to fence many enemies, ride strange horses, swim, run and shoot to survive.

He believed the event would test 'a man's moral qualities as much as his physical resources and skills, producing thereby the ideal, complete athlete'. He was so chuffed when the Modern Pentathlon was voted in as a sport, he exclaimed: 'the Holy Ghost of sport illuminated my colleagues and they accepted a competition to which I attach great importance'.

Nowadays, his baby doesn't command the same airtime as de Coubertin once hoped, but it is still very impressive to watch, with an exciting climax to boot. Competitors take on all the others in a one-off fencing match (épée), with the first to score a hit winning the fight. If neither manages within a minute, they both lose. They then swim 200m freestyle as fast as possible. Next, the hosts provide a stable of similar horses, and the athletes draw their steed randomly, so testing their ability to ride a new mount over an unfamiliar course of fences.

During these three preliminary events, the athletes build up a score, which is translated into a head-start for the final event: running and shooting combined. Therefore, the current leader might start several minutes before the current back marker. Along the route, the athletes must shoot down targets with a pistol. Whoever makes it to the finishing line first wins gold.

ROWING

IF THERE WAS A PRIZE FOR 'MOST-POOPED-LOOKING' at the Olympic Games, then the rowers would be up against the decathletes and triathletes for gold medal. The medal-winning boats can usually force a smile or wave at the crowds once they cross the finishing line. But for the losers, the expression of physical exhaustion and abject misery that all their training over the last four years has brought them nothing more than a pat on the back, is written large.

The best teams will do the same stroke, over and over, harder and harder, in better synch than the others. There are two types: *sweep* (with one oar) and *sculling* (with two), split into lightweight (less than 72.5kg for men and 59kg for women) and heavyweight categories. The sweepers compete in pairs, fours and eights, while the scullers are individual, in doubles or quads. Some have coxes, some don't, but the goal is the same: get to the finishing line first and don't die wondering.

Boats tend to start fast, setting a quick, rhythmic stroke (about 40 per minute), then try to find enough in the tank to sprint for home. There is mental racing pressure from watching your opponents take a lead or fall behind. Do you trust your strategy or hit the panic button?

Talk a good game

Catch a crab: To make a faulty stroke, and send yourself and the *shell* (boat) off balance. The loss of time and rhythm can prove costly.

Coxswain (cox): The mouthy little fella or lass in the shell who faces in the direction of travel and barks orders at the giants pulling on oars. Coxes steer too, and often get thrown in the drink if the team wins. Derives from *cockboat* (a small boat on a ship, like a lifeboat) and *swain* (a servant), although there's only one person in charge nowadays.

'He's put on a bit of weight since he rowed in the Olympics.'

Engine room: The colossal rowers in the middle of an eight, who provide the grunt.

Hammer: Someone who is appreciated more for their power than their finesse.

Stroke: Often the most technical rower, he or she sits closest to the stern and sets the rhythm for the others to follow.

Drunken octopus: When all the legs (i.e. oars) of an eight are moving to a different beat. Also, a *drunken spider.*

Puddles: Where the surface of the water is disturbed by the blades. You can get an idea of how well the boat is running by the distance of puddles from the stern.

Shooting your slide: When the seat slides ahead of your shoulders.

Bumps: Not an Olympic event, but it would be fun if it were! Boats leave at different time intervals, and the aim is to chase down the one in front, without being caught from behind.

SAILING

THE NAME OF THE GAME is to harness the power of the wind and cross the finishing line quicker than the other vessels. If this means changing your racing line to block others and gang up on the leader, then so much the better. There are different categories, with a number of different types of boat within each. With so much going on, the best way of explaining is to jump straight in.

Talk a good game

Match racing: This is one against one racing. There's a series of round robin matches, with the top teams progressing to the final knockout stages, culminating in a gold medal dogfight.

Fleet racing: This is a mass start, with many different boats racing round a course marked by buoys. Because of the variation of the wind, there are several races, so that the best sailor(s) emerge. You score one point for coming first in a race (and therefore 35 if you trail in 35th) and the lowest accumulated scores make the final race, where points scored are doubled. The one with the lowest points at the end of all that is the winner. As a result, in the final, the leader may only need to finish, say, third to win.

Windsurfing: This was nearly dropped from the Games in favour of kitesurfing, but then earned a reprieve. The best must come through a brutal schedule of races, picking up points to enter the medal race. Their rigs are called RS:X – a heavier design with a *daggerboard* (blade beneath the keel to improve stability) that aids racing in low wind (which can be useful, as the race start times are not dependent on wind strength).

470: So-named because it is 470cm in length, this is a two-man dinghy with a trapeze (so the sailors can hang off the side) and spinnaker sail, which blows out to aid speedy planing.

49er: A high performance two-handed skiff that can 'fly' at great speed across the surface of the water. Again the two-person crew can hang out the side. The hull is 499cm, hence the name. Women sail the 49erFX version, which is a slightly souped-up version, but pretty much the same rig.

Finn: Single-handed dinghy for the men, designated the heavyweight class, it is cat-rigged, with the sail at the front, which tests the basic sailing abilities and tactics to the max. This is a pure racing boat, with the best usually winning through devilry and skill. If you master the Finn, then you walk tall in sailing circles.

Laser: Lightweight and nippy, this was originally designed to travel on top of your car on weekend trips. A single sail, the operator needs to be hugely agile, strong and cutthroat in the heat of battle. Women sail the *Laser Radial*, which has a slightly smaller sail and doesn't demand the same brute strength.

Nacra 17: Catamarans are making a return to the Olympics, and the streamline Nacra 17 is the popular choice. Feeding off the popularity of the Americas Cup, this event has extra appeal in that the crews must be mixed, with both male and female sailors on board.

Gybing: To turn the boat across the wind, downwind.

Tacking: To turn the boat from side to side, using the eye of the wind.

Hiking out: Using the trapeze to lean over the side of the boat, and so balance it against the wind.

Yngling: An old Olympic class, and a great word! It's a keelboat. Yngling is the Danish for 'youngster' and was originally designed by Jan Herman Linge in 1967 for his young son. And it's pretty close to his surname too...

SHOOTING

THERE ARE THREE DISCIPLINES in the firearm sports – pistol shooting, rifle shooting and shotgun clay pigeon shooting. The first two are about amassing points through accurate target shooting with a single projectile; the latter is hitting moving targets with a pattern of lead shot.

Given all of the competitors are able to hit the centre of the target, and shoot down clay pigeons from every possible angle, this event is usually won between the ears, with the gold medallist able to maintain concentration and blank out the pressure of the situation. A bit like a martial artist, they can find a mental state of absolute focus – or flow – where nothing else exists other than the process of hitting the target. The ability to instantly forget a *lost* target and concentrate on the next is critical.

The rifle and pistol classes require shooters to fire bullets at a 10-ring target within a given time. The shotgunners fire at pairs of targets, released after their command.

Talk a good game:

Air pistol: The pellet is forced by compressed air from a 0.177 calibre pistol at targets 10m away.

Rapid fire pistol: Not exactly Dirty Harry, but it's possibly the most dramatic of the pistol events. With a .22 calibre over 25m, shooters (men only) have eight seconds to fire at two series of five targets, six seconds for two more series of five shots, and then four seconds for the last two series of five shots.

Free pistol: Longer distance shooting, again with a .22, but with stabilisers to avoid a shaky hand. Men shoot over 50m, women over 25m.

Air rifle: Like the air pistol, again over 10m, standing, but with a .22 calibre.

Shooters use open sights, rather than the telescopic sights more common in game hunting.

Long Rifle: This tests the shooter's ability to measure the wind speed and direction, with 40 shots apiece from a standing, kneeling and prone (lying) position. The best eight make the final, where they shoot off from a standing position. There's also a separate event for men, which is prone shooting only.

Trap Shooting: Often referred to as *ball trap* (ouch!) on the Continent, this is a popular longer-range event in which shooters line up and take it in turns to shoot targets flying away from them. There are lots of different traps that send out the clays, and you don't know where they are going to come from, although everybody gets the same combinations over 125 clays. In the qualification rounds, shooters can use both barrels, but just one for the six who make the final (another 25 clays). The highest score out of 150 wins.

Skeet: There's a bit more variety here, with clays crossing and coming in singles or pairs. Again, the shooters stand in a line, but this time in a semi-circle. The traps launch out the clays from either side, with only one barrel allowed per clay. Again, qualification leads to the final, with the highest score winning gold.

Double Trap: This is all about making your *left-and-rights* (hitting with both barrels). The clays are launched out from in front, always in couples, but at different heights and speeds. The shooters need to react within a split second, whilst maintaining focus and rhythm. Again, they take it in turns to shoot 25 couples, with three qualifying rounds and a final, making a total of 200.

TABLE TENNIS

THIS IS ANOTHER HOUSEHOLD FAVOURITE that we've all played, so getting a sense of what's actually going on isn't that tricky. But could we give the Olympians a game? No chance! Even if we could get a serve back in play, given the audacious speed, spin and deception, then we'd have less than half a second to adjust to the next shot to arrive with searing topspin. Happily, we can admire from afar, and then imitate at our own leisure.

Rallies tend to be decided on momentum. You get your opponent out of position – either with a good serve, evil spin or deception – then hammer away at this weakness until he or she makes an error. As in tennis, some players are excellent counter-punchers, able to soak up pressure defensively, wear out the aggressor and then launch a stinger of their own.

The rules are largely as you might expect. The ball has to bounce once on the opponent's side, crossing the net. Serves are the 'ping-pong' style, bouncing on both sides. There are slight differences in the Olympics from the game you likely play against family or friends. Players take it in turns to serve twice, rather than five. The serve must be dropped from an open palm, and games are the first to 11, with a two-point cushion, rather than 21. Best of seven games.

In doubles matches, you play alternate shots, and the serve must be from the right-hand corner to the player horizontally opposite. In the team events, each team consists of three players, who play four singles matches and one doubles match, like in a Davis Cup tie.

Games can get very noisy. Players will audibly celebrate each point, fist pumping all the way. At least that's one part of the game we can all match.

Talk a good game

Fake serve: Players try to anticipate the direction of the serve, so deception can draw them out of position. This delayed serve, through sleight of hand, does exactly that.

Shakehands: When you grip the handle of the bat like you are shaking hands. Favoured by Westerners.

Penhold: As the name suggests, the bat is controlled by the thumb and forefinger to give more spin. Preferred by Far Eastern players, who – let's be honest – know a thing or two about table tennis.

Chop: To return a top-spinner with backspin.

Counter-smash: When you smash back a smash. Take that!

Dead ball: To return without any spin, catching your opponent out.

Drop shot: Effective when your opponent is yards behind the table.

Gluing up: Bat rubbers are often attached at the last moment to improve performance.

Cho!: What the top players shout to celebrate a point. It's Mandarin for 'ball' and therefore short for *Hao Cho!* (a good ball). Celebrating a net cord or a poor shot by your opponent is deemed unsportsmanlike, but such is the excitement and pressure, many players can't contain themselves.

High toss serve: When the serve comes down from a height, so the server gets more spin. However, the server must toss the ball before striking it – simply dropping the ball or hitting it out of your hand makes it easier to generate more spin. Likewise, you can't hide the ball when serving – the receiver should be able to see how you are going to spin the ball.

Kill: A shot that's too fast for your opponent.

Loaded: Heavy with spin.

Paddle: Another name for the bat.

Funny rubbers: When the rubber surface of the bat has long *pips* or *pimples* to aid spin. In the Olympics, they can have smooth or pipped rubbers, depending on their style. If you have one of each, then you might *twiddle* the bat between points. Players can check to see which rubber their opponent is going to use before a match begins, although touching the rubber with your sweaty fingers is deemed very poor show.

'Great smash, partner...!'

TAEKWONDO

A RELATIVELY NEW MARTIAL ART, starting in South Korea in the 1940s, taekwondo is a perfect spectator sport as the goals are simple to explain. It literally means 'the art of foot and fist': the fighters gain points by kicking and punching. Scoring is similar to boxing and fencing: you need to hit the right bits of your opponent with sufficient force to register a point.

Bouts are across three rounds of two minutes, in a knock-out draw that leads to the gold medal match. A kick or punch to your opponent's torso scores one point, while you get two if it's a spinning kick. You can't punch to the head, but you can kick. Fighters are matched according to weight divisions.

Competitors need to have fast reactions, as points are usually scored by counter attacking. The ability to recover quickly from a blow is key, as even the best will get hit and bruised throughout a competition. And you need legs like a kangaroo.

Talk a good game

Like Japanese judo, there are plenty of strange Korean words, but here are some bankers:

Taekwonda: The fighter.

Dobok: The white uniform worn by everyone.

Deuk-jeom: A point.

Gam-jeom: A one-point penalty.

Chung: The contestant in the blue helmet and bib.

Hong: Their opponent in red.

Dollyo-Chagi: A roundhouse kick to the head, flying and spinning in mid-air. One for the photographers.

Naeryeo-Chagi: Axe kick. Like a karate chop, but with your leg on top of the head.

TRIATHLON

ONE OF THE WORLD'S FASTEST GROWING SPORTS, the triathlon – with its *Iron Man* big brother – is a mighty test of a competitor's stamina and willpower. The numbers themselves make for exhausting reading. Athletes need to swim for 1,500m in open water, cycle for 40km, then run a 10,000m course. No wonder they collapse over the finishing line. The winner has no puff left to celebrate.

The changeovers – involving the bike – can be crucial in the final reckoning, with smooth transitions saving time and infringements causing time penalties or even disqualification. It's rare for athletes to be especially strong in all three disciplines, so doing well in your weakest suit is often the key to winning. The swimming stage has a reputation for skulduggery – grabbing, unzipping, kicking – as it is so hard to monitor. The Olympic spirit goes on ice, until the swimmers spread out…

Talk a good game

Brick: A workout, practising two of the three disciplines.

Dolphin Dive: A series of short, shallow dives when running into breaking water.

Aero bars: Forward-facing handlebars with a groove for your elbows to aid aerodynamics.

Chamois Butter: A lubricant to wear under your shorts to avoid saddle sores, when you have a soggy bum after the swim.

Fartlek: Alternate fast and slow intervals to raise endurance.

BOP: Back of the pack competitor. *FOP* is at the front.

Rabbit: Someone to chase. It might be a good swimmer, who you aim to chase down before the finish.

WATER POLO

WATER POLO has a reputation for thuggery and violence, which is an essential part of its appeal. There is a huge skill level required to pass the ball up the *tank* (pool) and score in the nets. Think handball on water, with only 30 seconds allowed to score per play, so it's frenetic fare. But this is also a sport for hard nuts who can tread water for long periods, without ever touching the bottom or sides, and still find enough energy to whack or dunk their opponents.

Fighting in the cover of white water is commonplace, especially underwater where the officials can't see who did what. Compared to the good old days, however, modern water polo is but a splash in the park. Players are immediately called for 'brutality' if they punch or headbutt, and ejected for the rest of the match. If the same sanctions were levied on past Games, especially the infamous 'Blood in the Water' match between Hungary and the USSR in 1956, there would have been nobody left in the pool!

There are seven players, including a full-time goalkeeper, who protects a floating goal. Attacking players need to be able to swim quickly with short arm turns to protect the ball, while defenders back pedal with their torsos out of the water.

The Hungarians remain the superstars of the sport, which is something of a religion in their country.

Talk a good game

Dry pass: To throw the ball to a colleague out of the water. Only the goalie can catch the ball with two hands. A *wet pass* skims across the surface, and the player might swim onto it. A *wet shot* skims towards the goal.

Hole set: To throw the ball to a position in front of goal, where the striker has a chance of scoring.

Eggbeater: Like synchronised swimming, the players need to tread water with their upper bodies far above the surface.

Full-tank: To use the whole pool in a move.

Kickout: To be ejected.

Ball under: A foul called on a player for taking or holding the ball underwater when an opponent tackles the player.

Swim-off: Two players race for the ball in the centre to restart play.

Foul: These are either ordinary, like a ball under, or major, like interfering with a free throw when your mates are out of position. A *major* foul results in a 20-second exclusion, and good teams make the extra man count with a goal. Three majors is a permanent exclusion.

Caps: These are numbered to aid identification (of the guilty culprit), with ear protectors, presumably to stop them from being pulled off underwater.

Crash back: When the attacking team loses possession, and then swim back to their own end as quickly as possible.

Donut: To score between the goalie's outstretched arms. A lob shot drops just below the cross bar.

Dribbling: To swim with the ball.

Penalty throw: On the five metre line, awarded when a player was fouled in the act of shooting.

Sink: To dunk another player.

Splashing: A major foul if done intentionally to impede the player. Who me?

Tackling: Hold, sink, grab, pull – you can pretty much do what you like to a player in possession.

WEIGHTLIFTING

TO SAY THAT WEIGHTLIFTING IS ABOUT LIFTING WEIGHTS is a massive simplification. The strongest and most technical may often win, but there's a lot more to it than just strength and technique. There's an intriguing game of bluff at play too, with a side order of 'chicken'.

For the different weights – there are eight classifications for men between 56kg and over 105kg, and seven for women between 48kg and over 75kg – lifters must do both the *clean and jerk*, and the *snatch*. In the first, the barbell is lifted to the chest in a squat position, then heaved above the head. The second is one fluid motion from floor to above the head. Leg and core power is every bit as important as chest and arms. Explosive power beats raw strength.

Only when the judges believe the lifters are holding the barbell with locked arms and straight legs will the buzzer sound, and the competitors can then throw the weight to the ground in relief or nonchalant disdain, depending on their poker face. Your combined best lift from each discipline makes up your final score, with the highest combined score taking gold. If there's a tie, then the lighter athlete wins.

So, surely the strongest on the day wins? Not always. The mental side of weightlifting is key. Locker rooms are full of athletes and coaches yelling and slapping each other to motivate themselves and out-psych opponents. The key thing to remember is that the weight on the bar always goes up – it can't stay the same or go down. Lifting a weight before your opponent puts the pressure on them. You may choose to try a weight at the edge of your ability, in a bid to make your opponent go first and bomb out, or force them to nominate a higher weight still.

Recovery time is also a consideration. So, if even if you fail, you might nominate a higher weight for your next lift to avoid going again before your opponent. Eventually, you will need to record a weight to get your final score, but you might be able to nobble your opponent in the process.

Talk a good game

Knurling: This is the criss-cross etching on the bar to give grip.

Sleeve rotation: For Olympic lifting, the weights at each end are free-moving and rotate as the weight is lifted. They would be much harder to lift if they didn't, as the lifter would need to release their grip.

Bumper plates: These are the weights, coated with rubber so that they bounce when dropped. 10kg is green, 15kg is yellow, 20kg is blue, and 25kg is red. As the weight may go up by just a kilo, there are *iron plates* – 0.5kg is white, 1kg is green, 1.5kg is yellow, 2kg is blue, 2.5kg is red, 5kg is white again.

Collars: The plates are secured by collars that weigh exactly 2.5kg each.

Clean: This is the initial movement, lifting the barbell up to your shoulders from a squat position.

Jerk: The completion move. One leg shoots backwards and the barbell is heaved up above the head in a rapid movement, where it is (hopefully) caught cleanly and held aloft with arms locked.

Snatch: The lifter brings the barbell up above his head into a squat, before straightening his legs to complete the lift and get three white lights.

Hang: When the bar is lifted just above the knee in a preliminary movement.

Power: A partial squat position – a potential tipping point where the lifter will drive on or fail.

Chalk: The white powder on the hands and often the neck to avoid the bar slipping. Gives grip and avoids moisture from sweaty palms.

Belt: Lifters may wear a belt of 12cm to provide support to the lower back.

Raised heel: Weightlifting shoes have a raised heel of about an inch to aid posture and gain a deeper squat.

Hook grip: Lifters hook their thumb around the bar, then enclose their thumb with their fingers, rather than leave it out the side. It's much more secure, but also leads to severe callousing, so their thumbs are usually heavily taped.

WRESTLING

WRESTLING IS ABOUT AS OLD A SPORT AS THERE IS, not least as you don't need any kit to do it, save for a circle drawn in the dirt. At the Olympics, the bouts are better organised with a mat, referees and proper clothing, but the basic concept remains: whoever can grapple their opponent into submission, pinning their shoulders to the ground, is the champion. In freestyle wrestling, the whole body is in play. In Greco-Roman wrestling, which is just for men, contact is above the waist only.

Divided by weight, there are bouts of three two-minute periods, with just 30 seconds between. If wrestlers achieve a pin – forcing the opponent's shoulders down for two seconds – then this is like an ippon in judo, with immediate victory. Otherwise, they try to amass points with various throws and take-down moves. The more spectacular the better. Two well-matched wrestlers will often grind into a stalemate, with just the rare point separating them. Famously, in 1912, a bout between a Russian and Finn lasted 11 hours. Time limits were instated soon afterwards.

Alongside brute strength, competitors need speed of mind and limb, using their opponent's momentum and weight against them with a sudden counter-attack.

Talk a good game

Body lock: To wrap your arms round an opponent, then throw them to the ground.

Bridge: To arch your back so that it isn't touching the ground and therefore giving a point away.

Arm throw: A fireman's lift, but where the fireman throws you on your back and then jumps on you.

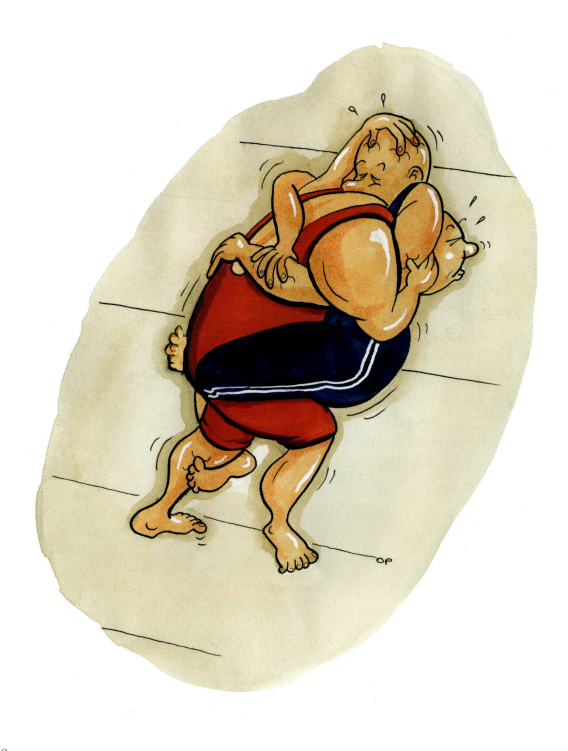

Take-down: To grapple your opponent to the ground from a standing start.

Gambit: A move to attempt to gain control. In chess it is sacrificing a pawn to gain control, but the term originates in wrestling. From the Italian *gambetto*, a trip to gain an advantage. An opening gambit in conversation moves the discussion in the direction you want.

No holds barred: When anything goes. Doesn't happen at the Olympics, of course, but it's a lovely phrase and it comes from wrestling.

The clinch: Typical of Greco-Roman wrestling, the fighters grapple in a standing position.

Go to the mat: To wrestle. Has passed into business speak where it means to take on an opponent in a dispute.

Fat: Self-deprecating comment by a wrestler to admit they are above their weight category. They could be 'two pounds too fat'. Just don't shout it from the stands.

Fish: Disparaging term for a wrestler that flaps about on the deck without a great deal of skill or tactics.

Gassed: When the wrestler is pooped.

Homerun: A Hail Mary in other sports. When you're losing, you try a risky move to get a pin.

Mat time: Experience. No substitute for it.

Stick: To pin.

Stud: Term of praise for a good wrestler.

WINTER OLYMPICS

THE WINTER OLYMPICS are often viewed as the younger sibling of the summer Games, but they originated at a similar time under the title of Nordic Games. Indeed, their trailblazer was a good friend of Baron Pierre de Coubertin and a founding member of the International Olympic Committee: General Viktor Gustav Balck. This devoted Swede also saw an opportunity to boost his home country's profile, so the early Games were all held in Sweden or Norway, which was in union with Sweden at the time. In 1924, the Winter Olympics were officially launched, and Chamonix held the first IOC-sanctioned jamboree.

They too have had their troubles – not least from opportunist politicians and performance-enhancing drug cheats – but several Games also found themselves at the mercy of unseasonal weather. At least modern organisers can create the necessary snow and ice if nature doesn't oblige.

Part of their captivation for the spectator comes with the danger element that accompanies most of the Winter sports. Downhillers battling for control, ski jumpers soaring over 100m, figure skaters flipping and spinning, freestyle skiers and snowboarders somersaulting high in the night sky, skeleton bobbers and lugists propelling themselves down an ice tunnel on a tea tray: they are all just split seconds from something very nasty indeed. No wonder, we can't take our eyes off their every move.

'Can you wait till the last racer has cleared the course?'

ALPINE

FOR ANYONE WITH A LOVE OF THE MOUNTAINS, the alpine events at the Olympics are essential viewing. From the aggressive power of downhill and Super-G to the more technical precision of slalom and giant slalom, the basic aim is the same: get to the bottom faster than the other skiers on the day and you'll never need to buy a drink in your home resort ever again.

Amid all the glory runs and moments of blistering drama, alpine brings plenty of misery too for its competitors. Every Games brings spectacular wipe-outs and plenty of giant-toppling, as firm favourites go away empty handed. But who wants sport to be predictable?

There are five ski disciplines: downhill and super-G are pure speed events. Slalom and giant slalom are more about precise turning around a series of gates, while super combined is an all-round test.

Talk a good game:

Downhill: Arguably the blue riband event at the Winter Olympics. Men and women in skin-tight suits reach speeds of 70 – 80mph on skis, with assorted jumps, tucks and battling turns.

Super-G: Super Giant Slalom. The gates are slightly tighter and more frequent, but this is basically a second downhill, with the same emphasis on attack and power.

Slalom: Originally a Norwegian word meaning 'a gently-sloping track', modern slalom racing is anything but gentle. The competitors zigzag through tightly-packed spring-loaded gates. Racers go twice, with the first-round leader going last to maximise drama.

Giant Slalom: Another technical event, but the gates are positioned further apart.

Super-Combined: A test to find the best speed and technical skier. Competitors complete both a downhill and slalom course on the same day, with the lowest aggregate time the winner.

Split times: The course is split into different sections, so the viewer knows if the racer is on the pace. When the little '1' pops up on the screen, we have a new leader, even by a hundredth of a second. Will they still have a '1' at the end?

Cowbells: It's hard to clap loudly with mittens on. You'll hear these herd bells tolling to encourage the racers, alongside the traditional 'hup-hup-hup'. Started in the Alps, but now a global phenomenon. Is there any lovelier noise in the summer than the gentle music of milk cows on an Alpine meadow?

Aprés Ski: The evening's entertainment, after the skiing has ended. Often starts at lunchtime, if the snow or viz is bad.

Brain bucket: A helmet. No excuse for not wearing one nowadays.

Chocolate Chips: Little rocks peaking through the snow.

Chowder: Chopped-up powder.

Corduroy: Just after the snow plough has done its thing, the snow looks like your great uncle's trousers.

Couloir: A narrow pass with nasty rocky faces on both sides.

Flat Light: When the grey light makes it hard to pick out where the sky ends and the slope starts.

Pow Pow: Powder. Usually said with great excitement.

CROSS COUNTRY SKIING

ALMOST AS OLD AS THE HILLS and forests it covers, cross country is the purist's skiing and a way of life for those who love it. The best enter a Zen-like state, able to glide at high speeds across several valleys without slowing up. Some events are up to 50km long.

In the biathlon, competitors need to shoot targets along the way. A fascinating event, invented by the Norwegian military in the 18th century, that tests technical accuracy under extreme levels of fatigue. Each station has five small targets – both prone and standing – which they must shoot with open sights rifles, carried on their backs. If they miss, then competitors get time penalties, or they're made to do additional 150m loops, just to make them even more tired. There are several different races, including the exciting mixed relay to find the leading nation. Hint: it's likely to be Norway.

Talk a good game

Classic: The classic cross country skiing technique along groomed parallel tracks, in which the skiers slide gracefully forward, lifting their heel as they kick the ski forward with their toes.

Freestyle: Looks more like ice skating and is much faster. In the relays, teams must use a combination of both classic and freestyle.

Melon Slide: Face planting in the snow. Also *nose-burner*.

Pin Head: A telemark skier, who wears 3-pin bindings.

Sitzmark: German expression for a 'bum mark' in the snow, where the unfortunate skier has veered off the track.

Skins: When you put a material – traditionally animal skin – on the bottom of your skis, so you can climb uphill quicker. *Skinning* is also used by off-piste alpine skiers.

Telemark: Very elegant if done well, the skier comes down hill on cross country boot bindings, bending one leg as they turn.

Diet sticks: Term for the skinny cross country skis. It's a good way to burn off the blubber too.

Misery sticks: Derogatory term for skis when the skier isn't having a good time.

Yard sale: Term used by skiers and cyclists alike. To have a mega crash, so that there are bits of equipment strewn everywhere.

Nord: Short for *nordic*. A cross-country or telemark skier.

Forest fairy: Lovely expression to describe the early morning tracks left by a super-keen skier who has been there and long since gone.

Shoot clean: Hitting all your targets in biathlon without incurring penalty points.

CURLING

CURLING IS OFTEN DESCRIBED AS LAWN BOWLS ON ICE, which works to a certain extent. After all, the aim is to throw more of your missiles closer to a target than your opponent. But the teamwork aspect to curling, not to mention the physical challenge of sweeping the stones, brings a deeper level of intrigue and drama.

In teams of four, each player throws two 42-pound stones apiece at the *house*, the scoring area (12 feet in diameter) at the other end of the rink (about 140 feet away). There are ten ends in the match, and you score points by having the closest stone to the centre of the house. If you have three closer, say, then you score three points. But the stone must have some part in the house to score.

The *skip* calls the shots, and then throws the final – and usually decisive – pair of stones. Whichever team has the *hammer* throws last, giving them the best chance of scoring. If you score, then the hammer passes over, so restricting your opponents to a single point is a good play. The brushing is critical, as it warms up the ice in front of the stone, lessening friction and so causing it to curl less than it would, and also slide further, if needed. So, curling is extremely vocal, with players urging their teammates to sweep harder or lay off.

The 10 qualifying nations play each other once, with the top four advancing to the semi-finals.

Talk a good game

Backline: The end of the ice. If stones cross this line, they are removed.

Take-out: To knock your opponent's stone out the way. Just hitting it isn't enough, you need to ensure it doesn't ricochet off in a hazardous way.

'What are you two looking so smug about?'

Blank end: When no points are scored. A team might deliberately choose to blank an end, as they will retain the hammer.

Steal: To score a point without having the hammer.

Counter: A stone in the house, and therefore a possible point scorer.

Draw weight: The right speed to stop where the curler wants it to.

Easy: A call from the skip to sweep lightly.

Gripper: A strip of rubber on the curler's shoe so they can both slide forward and stop.

Burned stone: When a stone is touched by a brush in motion, it is then discarded. Honest curlers will admit to this.

Hurry!: When the skip wants his or her cohorts to sweep hard. Also: *Hard!* Or even *hurry hard!*

Off!: Stop sweeping! Also: *Right off!* Whoa!

Biter: A stone that's just touching the outer circle of the house.

Kizzle kazzle: The surface of the rink is *pebbled* (sprayed with water to make it bobbly), and sometimes slushier as the game goes on. This is when the curler deliberately wobbles the stone to make it run smoother.

Stacking the brooms: Colloquial term for having a drink after the match.

Guard: In the early stages of the end, teams will place and remove guards – blockers – to gain an advantage.

Figure Skating

IS THERE A MORE GRACEFUL SIGHT IN SPORT than figure skating? Whether individually or in pairs, the skaters perform their series of jumps, spins and fancy footwork at high speed. Any mistake results in lost points. Any fall on the hard ice is met by millions of gasps from viewers on their soft sofas worldwide.

Skaters perform two routines – the technical elements and then the freestyle dance routine, which gives them more freedom to express themselves and put on a show. Nine judges score them on choreography and technical proficiency.

The name 'figure skating' harks back to the days when skaters were judged on their ability to etch perfect figures in the ice with their skates. Nowadays, it's the jumps and spins that win most points and hearts. There are six main jumps – three using the toe pick (metal teeth at the front of skate) to jump, and three just using the edge of the blade, and therefore more difficult. The blades have a groove down the middle called the hollow, which allows skaters to skate on the outside or inside edge, and get more purchase. Depending on which edge they use, the difficulty of the jump changes.

Talk a good game

Mohawk: When skating forward, you spin from one foot to the other, so that you end up going backwards. Often used as a prelude to a jump, as five of the six jumps start and finish from a backward-facing position. Only the Axel starts from a forward-facing position.

    1. Loop: An edge jump that starts off the back outside edge and lands on the back outside edge of the same foot.

    2. Toe Loop: A loop, but using the toe pick to jump.

'One can't help but feel she should have stuck to hurdling.'

3. Salchow: Named after Ulrich Salchow, a star Swedish skater in the first decade of the 20th Century, this is an edge jump that starts from the back inside edge and lands on the back outside edge of the opposite foot. A *triple Salchow* would have three turns.

4. Flip: Another toe jump, the take off begins from the back inside edge and is landed with the opposite foot.

5. Lutz: Named after Austrian pre-War maestro Alois Lutz, this is basically the same as a Flip, but more tricky as the skater takes off from the back outside edge instead. This makes the jump counter-rotated, meaning that the rotation of the jump is the opposite of its entry. A *Flutz* is a Lutz that becomes a Flip at the last moment, often because the skater suffers a confidence crisis.

6. Axel: Named after 19th Century Norwegian skater Axel Paulson (a Paulson wouldn't sound anything like as good!), this is the hardest jump and therefore the most likely to go wrong, although it may score you most points. It's easy to spot, as it's the only jump attempted whilst facing forward. All the power must come from the knees, through the edges, as the skater spins round to land going backwards again. That's another reason the fabled *triple Axel* is so difficult, as it is really a 3.5 turn.

Quad: A quadruple spin, which brings big points but also big crashes. Nobody has ever attempted or completed a *quad Axel* in the Olympics. Quads in other jumps are now quite common, so the quintuple is the new goal.

Waxel: An Axel that ends up on the ice.

Shoot the duck: To spin on one bent leg, holding the other foot out in front of you.

Kiss and cry: The booth where the skaters receive their awards.

Death spiral: When the man holds the lady by the hand and she spins round the ice in a circle around him, parallel to the ice, somehow gripping in with one blade.

WINTER OLYMPICS

FREESTYLE SKIING

THE GREATEST TRICKSTERS ON SKIS, freestylers navigate a range of artificial courses, with the fastest or most stylish declared the winner. In the Games, there are five medals up for grabs (as well as spins, jumps, grinds and flips). Snowboarding was once seen as an evolution of alpine skiing. Now it has returned the favour, as freestyle skiing owes much of its development to snowboarding.

Aerials: This is a cross between ski jumping and trampolining. The skiers launch themselves skywards from a concave jump and perform a routine of flips and somersaults while they're up there. Unlike the trampolinists, they must then land on two strips of thin carbon fibre.

Moguls: For skiers with rubber knees. They bounce down a field of 4ft high bumps at a rate of knots. The course also has two jumps, where the skier does a quick trick, then carries on down the moguls. They are judged for technical ability, speed and artistic merit. In *Dual Moguls*, which aren't currently in the Olympics, skiers race each other down, leading to epic falls. The word was originally 'mugel', a small hill in Bavarian German.

Ski Cross: One of the highlights of modern Games, this is basically a downhill – with lots of jumps and tucks – but congested into a four-skier race, so there is every opportunity for blocking and crashing. The first across the line is the winner, even if they're on their backside.

Halfpipe: Inspired by skateboarding and snowboarding, skiers perform their gnarly tricks down the tunnel. Each skier gets two runs, with the highest score counting, before 12 go through to the final. They then get another two. The winner will execute the most difficult jumps perfectly.

Slopeside: Imagine skateboarders and BMX riders in urban terrain parks – with rails and ramps – then put them on skis and drop them in the mountains. Contenders are judged on style, execution, difficulty and height.

Talk a good game

Like snowboarding, a whole new language has grown around freestyle skiing. Here's some of the most common phrases.

Backscratcher: To touch your back with the backs of your skis. Cossack: The skier spreads into a flying 'H' with hands down, legs out to the side and skis straight at the sky. Daffy: One leg straight in front with the ski pointing up, the other straight behind, with the ski pointing down. Helicopter: To spin 360 degrees. A *heli*.

Iron Cross: To create a perfect cross with your skis under your bum.

Mule Kick: To kick your feet up to the side, keeping your skis together.

Spread Eagle: To create a four-point star in the sky, with arms and legs akimbo.

Butter: To ski a section very smoothly.

Hole-shot: Take the lead from the start in ski cross and holding on to win the race.

Sling-shot: Using the draft of another skier to overtake them.

Working: To gain speed through the *rollers* (small jumps) on ski cross. Also called *pumping* or *milking*.

Grab: To grab any part of the ski whilst jumping.

Grind: To slide down a rail on your skis

ICE HOCKEY

FAST, PHYSICAL, IMMENSELY SKILFUL AND ENTERTAINING, each match has three 20-minute periods, and the idea is to put the puck in the net of your opponents and stop them doing the same to you. The best players need to be big and tough, as no matter how fast you skate, you will get body checked into the side boards on a regular basis.

Each team may have up to five players and a goaltender on the ice at any one time, but players can sub on and off whenever they like, including all five at a go if it's safe to do so. Most of the violence is legal, but when players overstep the mark, they'll be sent to the penalty box for two minutes (minor) or five minutes (major). A lot of goals are scored in this *powerplay* period, when one team has an extra player on the ice.

When teams are tied after regular time, then matches enter an overtime period: first goal wins, four against four. If that doesn't split them, then they play a shootout – like penalty kicks in football.

Talk a good game

Biscuit in the basket: To put the puck in the net.

Boarding: You can check players, but only if they have a chance to defend themselves. If you smash into their backs from behind, whiplashing them into the boards, that's not OK. Penalty.

Butt-ending: You can't jab them with the knob of your stick either.

Elbowing: Nor elbow them in the face. Nor slash, knee, trip or spear them, while we're at it.

Pull the goalie: If teams are a score down with a minute left, they might pull the goalie to gain a one-man advantage. This leaves the net empty, so a decisive goal could be scored from the other end.

Faceoff: Restarts are taken by dropping the puck between two players, who try to scoop it back to their teammate behind.

Line brawl: A fight between all the players on the ice.

Drop the gloves: When two players agree to have a fist fight by throwing off their gloves.

Shorthanded: To blank the opposition while defending a powerplay. Momentum shifts in your favour.

Icing: If you're defending a lead, say, you can't just keep dumping the puck to the other end to kill the clock. The official calls 'icing' and play restarts back at your end.

Offside: This is to stop goal hanging. You can't enter the offensive zone (by crossing the Blue Line) before the puck. If the puck exits the offensive zone, then all the attackers must too, before it re-enters.

Penalty shot: When a player is fouled in the act of trying to score, then he is given the puck at the halfway line and it's one on one against the goaltender.

A slapshot: A hard shot by jamming the stick into the ice behind the puck and using the energy from the bending stick to slap the puck goalwards at speeds of up to 100 mph.

Stand on his head: When a goalie plays so well that his underperforming team still win.

Sunburn: When a goal is scored, a light shines behind the goalie. If this happens a lot, he is in danger of getting sunburnt.

Ski Jumping

IMAGINE SITTING AT THE TOP OF THE RAMP with a vast crowd below, with over 100m of open hill between you and where you are supposed to land. You need to be slightly insane, or a phenomenal athlete to let go of the safety bar. Jumpers reach speeds of over 60 mph down the ramp and then fly further than a football pitch, before landing like a butterfly. These birds deserve all the kudos they get.

The Norwegians and Finns have a proud history in the event, as do the Japanese. In the race to fly further and smoother – a bit like jockeys, sprinters, racing drivers or swimmers – there is a constant battle between technology, human nature, commercial enterprise and the officials trying to keep everybody safe and entertained. Not an easy balance, but it's great to watch.

Talk a good game

Inrun: This is the steep track where the jumper gathers speed for take off. The organisers start them at the optimal and safest place. The tower is often referred to as the *scaffold*, which seems about right.

K-Point: A line in the snow that signifies a good jump. This is like par in golf – you've done well, but you'll probably lose to a birdie. Distance points are awarded for how far you fly beyond the K-Point. Interestingly, the K-Point is also the safest place to land, just as the slope is easing off. Beyond the K is the *breaking zone*, where you can win but also come a cropper.

Large hill: The big daddy for ski jumpers, where the K-Point is usually at least 100m and jumpers will fly much further than that.

Normal hill: The smaller hill – the K-Point can be as 'short' as 75m.

'Is that ALL we've got?'

Takeoff: Where the inrun ends and the skier takes flight. They launch their bodies forward, so they are leaning over their skis.

V-Style: The distinctive position of a ski jumper, with their skis forming a V to increase wind resistance.

Style points: Skiers lose marks, out of a possible 20, for any stylistic errors.

Telemark position: Skiers land with one knee bent, arms out and hands facing upwards. They are judged for artistic style.

Nordic Combined: This specialist event, which has its own medals at the Games, combines ski jumping and cross country skiing. The jump is first, with the best jumpers being given a headstart off. Whoever crosses the line first wins, and can probably lay claim to be the toughest dude at the Olympics.

SLEDGING EVENTS

THEY ARE INDIVIDUAL EVENTS in the Olympics, but bobsleigh, luge and skeleton bob are effectively grown-up sledging races. And just like we all do as kids when there's a good hill and enough snow, we go down as fast as we possibly can – either head first (skeleton), feet first (luge) or with several crammed on the same sledge (bobsleigh). The person at the back pushes, the one at the front steers as best they can. Admittedly, we don't have to navigate ice tunnels at speeds of close to 100 mph. But the principle is the same.

Bobsleigh: Teams of two or four navigate a twisting ice track, gathering speed with a sprint start. The pilot is in charge of steering these torpedoes, helped by teammates shifting their weight during corners. Each team gets four runs down the 1.5 kilometre track, but it can still come down to a hundredth of a second between glory and devastation.

Luge: In this singles or doubles slide fest, the loonies go down feet first on their tea trays at over 80 mph. Steering is down to slight body movements. Get it wrong and competitors will lose a thousandth of a second, or crash horribly. To stop, they have to use spikes on their feet. A fast start – sprinting and then bedding onto the luge – is critical, especially in the doubles. In the mixed relay event, individual men and women race, with men's doubles sorting out the medals.

Skeleton bob: Just when you think it couldn't get any more dangerous, here come the skeleton bobbers! The name refers to the bony-looking sledge, but there is a ghoulish ring to it. Inspired by the Cresta Run (hare-brained Brits hammering down the streets of St Moritz in Switzerland), the sliders go head first, again at speeds over 80 mph. It must be something in the water, because Britain is one of the sport's superpowers, and it's not often we can say that in the Winters.

Talk a good game

Labyrinth: a combination of three-turns.

Line: Like in racing driving, this is the fastest line through a corner.

Pushers: In the four-man sled, two additional athletes help push the sled and then sit in the sled between the pilot and brakeman.

Lip: The safety barrier at the top of the track to stop a sled spinning out into the crowd.

Rodel: German for sled. The Germans love this sport.

Loading: Getting into the sled after the sprint at the start.

Lose your head: The sliders face huge G-force pressures through their necks. If it proves too much, their head is pushed down and they struggle to see the path ahead.

Runner: The blades beneath the sled.

Pilot: Driver of the sled. Controls the two front runners on the sled, which include approximately eight centimetres of lateral movement via an attached rope, allowing the driver to steer the sled.

Brakeman: Sits at the back of the sled and controls the speed by applying the brakes at appropriate times. Brake handles are located on either side of the brakeman in a four-man sled and in front of the brakeman in the two-man sled.

SNOWBOARDING

ALTHOUGH STILL A RELATIVELY YOUNG SPORT, snowboarding is already part of the furniture at the Winter Olympics, and probably one of the biggest parties at the Games. The ultimate event is the *halfpipe*, where competitors pull outrageous tricks while zigzagging back and forward – and yards up above – the tunnel. Slopeside brings in much of the same acrobatics and showmanship, as boarders grind obstacles and rails, as well as some big air jumps.

There are more traditional alpine-looking events like the *parallel slalom* and *parallel giant slalom*, although it's head-to-head, rather than against the clock, with two racers duelling in a knock-out.

Finally, *boardercross* – inspired by motocross and BMX – brings four boarders in a race down a course of jumps and hops, with plenty of tumbles along the way.

Talk a good game

Boned out: To make a trick or jump look even more stylish, often by fully extending legs or arms.

Beige: Something that's a bit wack. Could be bad weather, a tasteless drink, your date not turning up.

Crew: Your riding posse.

Eat snow: To face plant.

Regular: To ride the board with the left foot at the front. *Goofy* is right foot first and less common. If you flip your feet round, so the back of the board is leading, you're riding *switch*.

Bail: To pull out of a move at the last moment.

Fakie: To ride the board backwards from a regular stance. Slightly different from *switch*, although if you land an *ollie* fakie, you can still say *switch* and people know what you mean.

Frontside: To perform a trick facing forward. Often abbreviated to FS, ie FS 360. *Backside* is facing backwards. If you're *blindside*, then you need to twist your neck to see the obstacle.

Bonking: To hit an obstacle with your board, either on purpose or accidently.

Grommet: A young super-keen boarder.

Phat: Something extraordinary. For example, phat air, phat snow, phat tune

Banging: To do something really well. 'That was a banging backside rodeo. Totally boned out.'

Battleship: A rail in the park shaped a bit like a big boat.

Japan: A common type of grab, with the back arched.

Rolling down the windows: Madly twirling your arms to try to regain balance on a jump.

Ollie: A jump.

Pipe: The halfpipe.

Bro: What you get called when someone doesn't know your name. Or dude.

Broadway: Really good. Also: *sick, rad, wicked, gnarly, tits, jampiece, tight.*

Ragdoll: A rider who has *stacked* (crashed) and is rolling down the hill like a ragdoll.

Rip: To board well. Also *shred*.

Sauce: To slide on rails.

Speed Skating

THIS IS SPLIT INTO TWO DISCIPLINES: short and long track skating.

In short track, skaters race around an ice rink at high speed. It's hugely exciting and never over till it's over, as skaters can wipeout at any moment, and often do. The ability to weave in and out of opponents, find space, kick and then strike for home is similar to track cycling. It's a non-contact sport. In theory, at least.

Long track skating (often just called speed skating) is all about speed. Skaters aim to maintain a smooth rhythm around a 400m track. Their event is against the clock – like the pursuit in cycling. It looks almost effortless, as athletes with legs like piston engines glide across the ice at over 30mph. Their hands are either tucked behind their backs to aid aerodynamics or pumping by their sides to increase speed. With their network or fjords and canals, perhaps it's no surprise the Dutch are global powerhouses in speed skating.

Talk a good game

Breakaway: To try leave the rest of the pack behind in short track.

Charging: To undertake your opponent, but hit them illegally. Competitors are often disqualified or reinstated after the race.

Hand on the ice: To help maintain balance round a corner.

Jump: Sudden kick of speed to open or close up a gap.

Burn out: To go fast from the start to exhaust your opponents.

Right of way: The line of the leader. Those behind must go around or up the inside if they want to pass.

Safety padding: Tracks have large crash mats to avoid injury when the skaters spin out.

Turnover: How fast the skaters are stepping. A bit like cadence in cycling.

Air resistance: What stops the skaters going a lot faster. Their body position is therefore key.

Clap skate: Used in long-track, the heel detaches from the blade, allowing the edge to remain on the ice for longer.

Crossover: When a skater's legs crossover on turns – they can therefore power round rather than lose speed. Speed, speed, speed!

Final whistle

Thank you for reading. I leave you with the thoughts of two legends in their chosen field. Both could certainly talk a good game.

'We take life too lightly and sport too seriously.'

John Arlott (1914–91)
Cricket commentator

'Some people believe football is a matter of life and death.
I am very disappointed with that attitude.
I can assure you it is much, much more
important than that.'

Bill Shankly (1913–81)
Football manager